The Student Journalist
and
MAKING ADVERTISING PAY
FOR THE SCHOOL
PUBLICATION

THE STUDENT JOURNALIST AND

THE
STUDENT
JOURNALIST
GUIDE
SERIES

MAKING ADVERTISING PAY FOR THE SCHOOL PUBLICATION

by

GLEN WRIGHT, *B.A., M.J.*
Journalism Instructor, Berkeley (Calif.) High School

CHAPTER ON COLOR AND DRAWINGS BY

JOHN ROBY
Staff Artist, Salinas (Calif.) *Californian*

PUBLISHED BY

RICHARDS ROSEN
PRESS, INC.
NEW YORK

Standard Book Number: 8239-0123-8
Library of Congress Catalog Card Number: 68-10818
Dewey Decimal Classification: 371.42

Published in 1968 by Richards Rosen Press, Inc.
29 East 21st. Street, New York City, N.Y. 10010

Revised Edition

Manufactured in the United States of America

ABOUT THE AUTHOR

Glen Wright came to the teaching of journalism via the route best designed to qualify him for it—twenty-nine years as a practitioner of all phases of newspaper publishing and advertising agency operation. At Berkeley High School in California, he currently teaches classes in journalism which produce a profitable daily newspaper and the yearbook.

After being graduated from high school in Los Angeles, California, he chose a life of adventure instead of college, spending several years working as a newspaper reporter and exploring in South and Central America and then making his way around the world as a seaman. Returning to the United States, he worked as a reporter on the Omaha (Nebr.) *World Herald* and several other papers before moving into advertising. After managing the advertising departments of several California papers, he became partner and publisher of the Hayward *Daily Review,* founded the San Lorenzo *Sun,* and founded and operated an advertising agency.

Retiring from publishing in 1958, he decided on a second career as a teacher, obtaining a B.A. in Advertising from San Jose State College and an M.J. from the University of California. In 1965 he was Fulbright Lecturer in Journalism and Advertising at the University of Kabul, Afghanistan, and adviser to the government press ministry.

In addition to his teaching post, he is currently associate editor of the *Northern California Messenger* and contributor to *The Publisher's Auxiliary, Editor & Publisher, The Journalist's World, Saturday Review, New York Times, Foreign Service Journal* and the Copley News Service.

CONTENTS

BOOK I
HOW TO SELL ADVERTISING

BOOK II
HOW TO CONSTRUCT AND WRITE ADVERTISING

The Student Journalist
and
MAKING ADVERTISING PAY
FOR THE SCHOOL
PUBLICATION

BOOK ONE

How to Sell Advertising

Chapter 1

ADVERTISING PROMOTES FREEDOM OF THE PRESS

The contribution of advertising to the school publication is significant in a context other than that of producer of income.

Advertising makes possible freedom of the student press in the same way it does the professional press.

Financial independence leads to operational independence in many ways.

School administrators, especially boards of education, may be less apt to impose controls or permit unwarranted outside interference if the publication is paying its own way.

Student body governments often think they buy immunity from criticism in the press with the funds they provide as subsidy. More often than not, they do evade their responsibilities in this manner. But such a situation need not be tolerated by the editor who is free of subsidy.

He can argue with great force and effect from his position of financial independence for the right to represent the reader rather than the special interest.

Improvement of quality made possible by adequate finances is a powerful argument in favor of advertising as an element of a free press. The acceptance of the publication as an advertising medium is proof of its reader interest. This acceptance by the reader can in turn be attributed to the quality of editorial content, which ultimately derives from the free discussion of ideas therein.

The Function of Advertising is to Reveal

Advertising contributes most cogently to the educational process as the search for truth, which is discovered by the revelation that results from free discussion of ideas. To reveal is the primary function of advertising. By its very nature, advertising at its best (most informative) is the most frankly and honestly revealing of all forms of written expression.

Advertising Enhances Quality

A host of practical considerations adds weight to the idea of selling advertising in the school publication. The income makes possible improved typography, more and better illustrations, better paper, wider choice of formats and covers, even color. Many newspapers and yearbooks use profits for such equipment as cameras, drawing boards, art materials, and audio-visual supplies.

Ad revenue may make publications available to more readers, either by substituting for circulation income when this is impossible to obtain, or by augmenting it when insufficient. Ideally, the newspaper should be distributed free to everyone on campus, and the yearbook should be low-priced to insure its availability to all who desire it.

In effect, income produced by advertising sales makes for a larger, more complete publication, truly representative of the social matrix of which the school is a part. Such a publication, reflecting the activities of all segments of campus society, contributes to democratization; reflecting all viewpoints and presenting a wide variety of information, it is a vital supplementary instrument to the process of learning.

These short-term advantages of advertising are appealing, but philosophical principles are even more satisfying.

Advertising is a Social Force

Basically, advertising in its role of mass communicator and persuader is a social force that expands and strengthens the very economy that makes free and widespread education possible, just as it makes possible a free and widespread press. As a tool of the marketing process, it helps bring buyer and seller together. It is salesmanship in print, and it is just as effective in diffusing ideas as it is in selling merchandise and service. It is a stimulating influence in civilization because it is a revealer of facts: illustrations, detailed description, the maker, the seller, the price, retailing policy, conditions of utilization, and many more such data are the warp and woof of advertising. It is a revealer of cultural values as it makes known trends, fads, fashions, customs, techniques, styles, and mores. In this respect it is a shaper of popular standards, making possible a free and enlightened choice of action from a broad range of alternatives.

Thus advertising expresses the inquisitive, acquisitive, impatient spirit of the age, appealing to youth and serving as an accelerator of facts and values. It constantly admonishes to "see it today," "buy it now," "act at once." It glorifies the new and the different, the better, the more comfortable and convenient.

Advertising in print became very brassy in the early years of this century, following the trend toward "yellow" or sensational handling of news and opinion. In recent decades, however, it has joined the journalistic trend toward objectivity. The best modern advertising is nondirective. It aims to help people to buy more intelligently by being primarily informative.

As a bridge between undeveloped resources and satisfaction of human wants, and between buyer and seller, it is the thoroughfare of teacher and learner. Are not all these the closest of kin?

ADVERTISING BELONGS IN THE STUDENT PUBLICATION

Thus it is entirely logical that advertising be in the school publication. Students are buyers. Nationally, students have billions of dollars to spend.

According to Jack Lefler, writer for *Associated Press Business News,* "the market they make is a phenomenon of modern merchandising."

There are about 11,000,000 teen-age girls in the United States, with some $6,000,000,000 a year of their own to spend.

More than 9,000,000 boys (14- to 17-year-old "teen-men") have an estimated $16,000,000,000 expendable income. Boys have an advantage over girls as they can more easily augment their family allowances with after-school and weekend job earnings.

With the increase in the U.S. population between 1960 and 1970 estimated at 12 to 22 per cent, the number of free-spending 15- to 19-year-olds is expected to rise by more than 40 per cent by the end of the decade.

To be added to these totals are more millions of students older than 19 in colleges, universities, and technical schools.

The youth market is expected to grow sharply in the next ten years. Tuition Plan, Inc., an educational installment financing subsidiary of the C.I.T. Corporation, says that by 1976 the annual bill for college expenses will be $22,700,000,000, double the present level. By the same date about 10,000,000 students will be in college.

Observers note that these youngsters, unnoticed before World War II, have become a separate and distinct group in society; and merchants are no longer lumping their spending with that of the family, but making strong efforts to cater to them directly. They are being called the New Frontier of the economy. They most certainly are a new bonanza for commerce. They have a desire for new things, new experiences, new loyalties, and they are not willing to wait for them. They want and get them now.

In a study for *Seventeen* magazine, Eugene Gilbert Youth Research found that 618,000 girls bound for college as freshman spent an average of $468 each outfitting themselves. A group of 5,800,000 high-school girls spent $231 each getting ready for school. Young men of precollege age spend almost $600,000,000 on clothing in August and September alone, according to estimates by the Boys' Apparel Association. Sales of accessories, luggage, appliances, school supplies, and textbooks are equally spectacular. There is a brisk demand for watches. The Samsonite Corporation says young people are the largest single group of luggage buyers.

Producers of small appliances report mounting sales to youth of table and transistor radios, hair dryers, record players, and portable television sets. Typewriter sales are booming, and manufacturers attribute a large part of the increase to student purchasers.

Equally impressive gains have been registered by makers and sellers of such conventional school supplies as pencils, pens, notebooks, erasers, rulers, and staplers. Paper makers are hard put to keep up with demand, running well behind orders received back in the fall of 1966.

Demand for textbooks has been unparalleled. While some publishers report something like a 20 per cent increase in sales in 1966, others use such superlatives as "fabulous, best year in our history, fantastic!"

Schools themselves are important customers, too. A $400,000,000 market for computers in education by 1970 is forecast. New chairs, desks, and auditorium and gym seating and other paraphernalia cost $100,000,000 a year. Hot-lunch programs for elementary and high schools funnel $1,000,000,000 into food production channels.

Seeing youth not only as current buyers but as future adult customers, and aware of youth's brand-name consciousness, retailers are catering to the young in many ways. Some have special shops within departments, club rooms, and charge accounts. They direct a proportion of their advertising to young prospects and find them responsive to it.

Merchants, then, require advertising mediums that will reach this student market. Obviously, the most effective is the school publication if it is realistically conducted. That is, it should be distributed to every pupil at fixed and stated intervals, be timely and interesting in content, and not only accept advertising, but also solicit and produce it as actively as news and editorial copy.

Attitude is all-important. The adviser and staff must understand and accept the basic premise: Advertising must be of value to its purchaser, it must sell his product or service or foster good will toward his business, and the publication must be an unbiased instrument in this process.

Therefore, solicitation should not seek advertising as a "favor" or "support," or as any kind of subsidy. Nor should solicitation be made of anyone who has nothing to sell the publication's readers.

The basis for every solicitation should be a sincere desire to serve the best, most legitimate interests of the client, which should ultimately result in a knowledgeable effort to produce an ad that will attract attention to his message.

In such ways advertising should serve industry and commerce. To completely fulfill its mission as a desirable social instrument, however, it must also serve its readers. It must do something for them, make it worthwhile for them to read and act upon it.

Initially, then, it should deal principally with the goods and services most in demand by students. Ideally, the advertising content of a school publication should be a buyer's guide that will obviate the time and effort normally required for store-to-store shopping. The questions What? Where? How much? should be immediately and constantly answered. Beyond this, the advertising should be timely and specific.

Finally, the student reader is served by honoring laws concerning minors. This prohibits advertising of tobacco, liquor, certain drugs, "adult-only" movies, shows and night clubs, salacious literature, and the like.

Chapter 2

THERE IS A KIND OF ADVERTISING
FOR EVERY SELLING PURPOSE

YOU CANNOT SELL IT IF YOU GIVE IT AWAY

Advertising is an appeal to buy that is paid for, nonpersonal, factual, and directed to a group.

Legitimate advertising, the kind to which the reader may unreservedly respond, which he may believe and continually utilize to make living more convenient, is so designed and written as to differentiate* it clearly from the editorial and news content of the publication.

The day of the so-called "reader" ad, the kind written and designed to simulate a news story, is long gone as an effective retail sales agent. It never was nor will be ethical, except when clearly labeled "advertising," being an obvious attempt to deceive the reader into thinking it news of general interest.

Passing into limbo also is the day of free publicity. This device, again advertising disguised as news, sells little or no goods or services. Its proponents, the "moochers" of the free enterprise system, who mistakenly think it is beneficial because it is free, continue to flood editorial offices all over the land with publicity handouts, and it is no credit to the intelligence or morality of editors that a great many of them get printed.

Neither advertising managers nor readers are fooled, however. The former know they are being bilked out of deserved and needed revenue, and the latter that they are being crassly deceived. (See Appendix A, page 157.)

Retailers, who do the bulk of the country's business, dominate the

19

pages of the professional press with aboveboard, large-space advertising. They will do the same for the scholastic press if student journalists use professional techniques in dealing with them.

Therefore, it behooves the student to begin by learning the different kinds of advertising and why and how they are employed by retailers. These kinds fall into two broad categories: Institutional and Promotional.

INSTITUTIONAL ADVERTISING STRESSES THE GENERAL

The underlying principle of all advertising is to make known to the public the existence, location, policies, products, and services of the retailer.

The kind of advertising that emphasizes this purpose is known as institutional because it deals with abstractions and philosophies rather than the specifics of selling. It attempts to promote confidence in the advertiser, to enhance his prestige, on the theory that the degree of acceptance of his goods and services will be closely related to that of his company as an institution.

Another term for this kind of advertising is "good-will"; its appeal is based chiefly on the number and types of services rendered, the completeness and qualities of merchandise offered, and the alertness shown by the advertiser.

This factor of *alertness* is a most important ingredient of an institution, especially in highly competitive situations. The retailer who is first to detect fads, trends, and "good buys" and who leads in offering the corresponding goods and services profits not only financially but also reputationally.

Institutional advertising is the stock-in-trade of yearbooks, magazines, and other infrequently issued periodicals.

Institutional advertising is of two kinds: *Prestige* and *Service*.

PRESTIGE ADVERTISING STRESSES REPUTATION
AND ACHIEVEMENT

The dictionary defines prestige as "ascendancy derived from general admiration or esteem."

Possession of this attribute is desired by retailers not only because it is a source of self-satisfaction and pride, but also because it has pecuniary value.

Once a store has achieved prestige, it can reduce its promotional expenditures to the point of optimum profit.

Prestige develops from the character and personality of the business, and it is immeasurably enhanced by advertising. "Word of mouth," so heavily relied upon by past generations of retailers, has never sufficed in competitive situations and will suffice even less in the space age. "To sell is to tell," and this applies to the abstracts of achievement as well as to the concretes of merchandising.

Reticence is not the role for the retailer. His light must always shine. It will not only be hidden from sight when under a bushel, it will go out from lack of oxygen.

However, "brag" advertising does not enhance prestige; rather, it detracts from reputation and results in a lessening of the desired influence.

Prestige advertising differs not a whit in approach from that of merchandising: It must be specific and objective; it must be based on deeds, not promises; the pattern must fit the cloth.

The two most effective prestige advertising approaches are those that portray enterprise or alertness, and complete line or selection of merchandise or services. (See Figs. 1, 2, 3, 4.)

Enterprise Advertising Tells Customers
First About the Latest

The new, different, and most beneficial is always most intriguing to the customer; therefore, the retailer who is first, or in the vanguard of the first, to make the latest development in goods and services available to his customers and tells them about it in advertising gains both immediate and long-term competitive advantage.

Because of his busy routine, the retailer often overlooks many opportunities for enterprise promotion. Along with the alertness he exhibits in merchandising, this quality may characterize many of his management policies. Because these are most often inspired by self-interest, their benefits to the customer often go unheralded.

Examples are bookkeeping systems, store layout and modernization, personnel changes, credit plans, civic projects, and the like. The more obvious opportunities for prestige publicity are in merchandising, where style, quality, ingenuity, and a host of other specifics provide copy themes. (See Figs. 5-18.)

The alert advertising salesman will call the retailer's attention

Fig. 1

Enterprise, Style

Fig. 2

Fig. 3

Enterprise,
Complete line

Fig. 4

Fig. 5

Enterprise, Style

Fig. 6

Customer convenience

THE BON MARCHE BUDGET FLOOR

Downtown   **Northgate**

step along in style

For that sharp ivy-league look, college hi blazers will have you stepping along in style this season.

a. Lapel model **3** button style, 3 pockets, 100% wool. Blue, camel, black. Sizes 6-20.   **12.99 to 14.99**

b. Two button cardigan with slit pockets, taperline sleeves. Green, blue, black, red, navy. Sizes 6-20.   **12.99 to 14.99**

This ad was prepared for The Bon Marche by our retail advertising class.

Boys' Wear, Budget Floor, Downtown.
Lower Level, Northgate

Fig. 10 Enterprise, Style

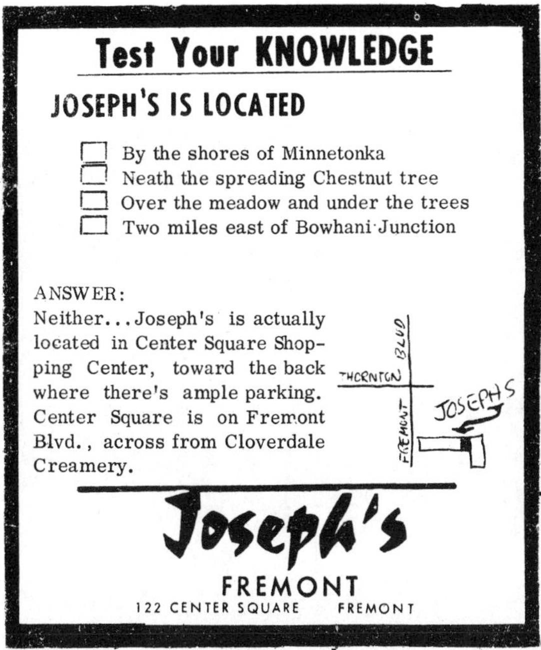

Fig. 11

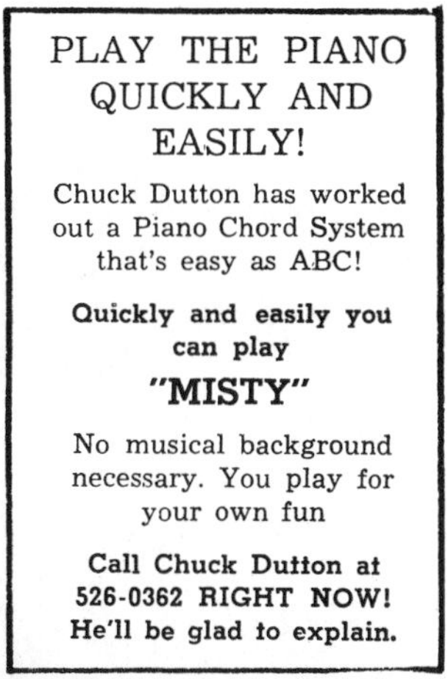

Fig. 12

Fig. 13

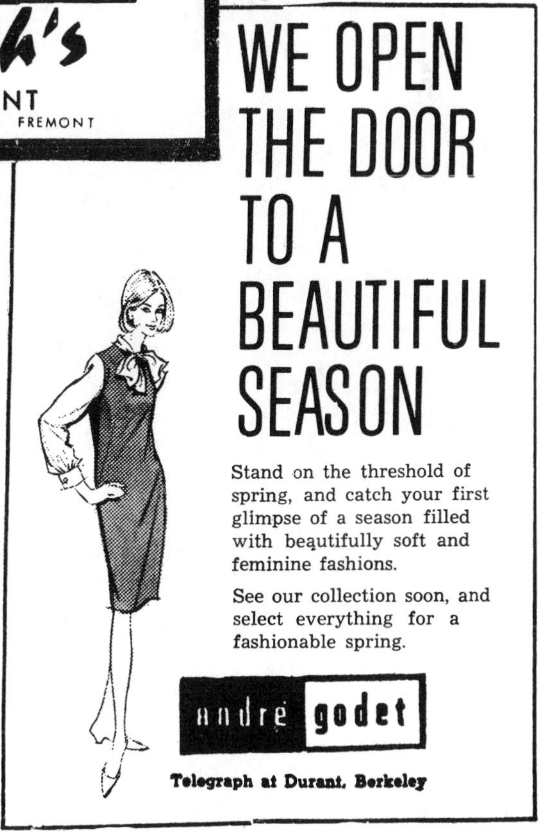

Fig. 14

Fig. 11 Service, Customer convenience

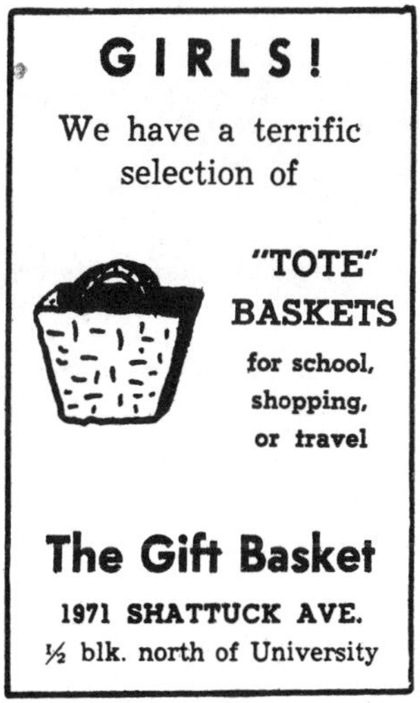

Fig. 12 News technique, Customer convenience

Fig. 13 Enterprise, Complete line

Fig. 14 Enterprise, Style

Fig. 17

Enterprise, Quality

Fig. 18

Enterprise, Style

to these many opportunities for enterprise advertising and obtain much extra business for his publication.

SERVICE ADVERTISING EMPHASIZES CUSTOMER CONVENIENCE

Customer convenience, in varying degrees, is the underlying theme of all good advertising. In service copy this theme predominates. The service ad is a "news" ad and is best written and laid out according to the rules for the summary-lead news story; that is, a general statement featuring the most important fact or idea, followed by supporting information in descending order of importance.

Only one subject should be discussed. Multiple-theme copy is difficult to write and, what is worse, difficult to read. For example, exposition of delivery service is a simple task, but explanation of complete line or array of goods and services can be complicated. The chore will be simplified if complete line is treated as singular.

However, the approach differs somewhat from that of the news story; being a commercial appeal, it is subjective. "You" and "we" are interrelated and involved: "*We* are doing thus and so for *your* benefit."

The headline should be in the active voice, and into it should be incorporated the customer benefit and the name of the store. If the copy is properly written, this can be taken from the first paragraph. Like many news writers, experienced advertising copy writers think in terms of the headline and write the lead to develop it. This technique should be used with caution, however, as it may lead to oversimplification.

All "reading ease" devices, such as short sentences and paragraphs, three periods (. . .) instead of semicolon, and dash (—) before enumerations and between phrases in apposition, should be used.

PROMOTIONAL ADVERTISING DOES THE DIRECT SELLING

The kind of advertising that does the selling, specifying item, price and conditions of the transaction, is called promotional.

For retailers promotional advertising is the most widely used. It is the principal support of newspapers and direct-mail publications such as catalogues and broadsides.

Inasmuch as the merchant must make a sufficient margin of profit to stay in business, most promotional advertising is *regular price line*; that is, it describes the merchandise or service, offers it at the going competitive price, and appeals for action within a seasonal time period.

The next most popular form is *bargain* or *special promotion,* which usually involves alertness or enterprise. The retailer manages to buy at a lower price than his competitors and advertises the goods at a lower price than they in a *special purchase* ad. The profit markup will remain the same as *regular price line.*

Or he devises a way to display and sell at a reduced cost and passes the saving along to the customer in the form of bargain prices. This kind of advertising is called *reduced from stock.* Again the normal markup percentage is maintained.

Less frequent but most flamboyant is *clearance* advertising. The retailer colloquially calls this the "dose of salts" that his store must take from time to time. It always involves selling for less than the usual markup and often for less than cost.

This necessity springs from "merchandise clog" caused by either over-buying or under-selling. In either case the retailer finds himself with too much goods, usually seasonal or faddish and becoming less salable by the day. To attract customers the merchandise is reduced in price and described in detail in clearance ads supplemented by special, vigorous in-store effort. (See Figs. 19-29.)

ADVERTISING CLASSIFICATIONS DEFINED

Display advertising is that which ranges in size from one column inch to a double-page spread in one layout, utilizing illustrations, border, and various sizes of type.

There are two kinds of display—*national* and *local;* two kinds of local—*retail* and *general;* and two kinds of classified (want-ads)— regular line copy and a combination called *classified-display,* which is simply display placed in the classified section.

National advertising is placed by manufacturers and wholesalers in newspapers and magazines and urges the reader to buy from the retailer or—in rare instances—from the advertiser.

Local advertising is placed by businesses in the trading area of the publication and seeks to sell directly to its readers.

Retail display is local display advertising by the retail store aimed at its particular segment of the market.

General advertising is local display of wide and unrestricted interest. It is mostly institutional and seldom includes a price. Bank

Shipped to us by
MISTAKE —
one shipment of classic furblend cardigan sweaters, light blue only.

Fig. 25   Reduced from stock

15% off while they last

Lyon's Casuals
Telegraph ave. at channing way

Fig. 26

Special purchase

HARRIS HOT BUY!

SPECIAL PURCHASE!
*very famous name
wash 'n wear*

PANTS

reg. 5.98
SPECIAL

3⁹⁹

Discontinued styles of collegiate Ivy Trims and Stags. Of long-wearing bulldog flannel, cotton gabardine or slim corduroy. Cambridge gray, loden green, char gray, black, sand, cactus and plaids.

HARRIS
OF BERKELEY

Shattuck at University
Open Thurs. nite to 9 • TH 1-1955

Fig. 27

Regular price line

Fig. 28

Regular price line

Fig. 29

Clearance

Fig. 30   upper left

National

Fig. 31   upper right

Local general

Fig. 32   above

Local retail

Fig. 33   left

Local retail

Fig. 34   right, upper

Classified-display

Fig. 35   right, lower

Classified

GET MORE OUT OF LIFE WITH GOOD VISION

The following Optometrists are sponsoring this message.

BERNHARDT N. THAL
2106 Shattuck
THornwall 5-4448

EDWARD MOGERMAN
3288 Adeline
OLympic 2-7621

HENRY TAKAHASHI
2414 Shattuck
THornwall 3-1228

E. TSUCHIDA
1535 Ashby Ave.
THornwall 3-8169

HAROLD ZLOT
190 El Cerrito Plaza
LAndscape 6-2242

SIGMUND D. SABIN
2124 Center Street
THornwall 1-1674

FRED W. STARRATT
2161 Allston Way
THornwall 3-2897

NATHANIEL S. WEST
2132 Center Street
THornwall 3-9068

Fig. 36

National Better Vision Week

SPECIAL EVENTS

Fig. 36a   Halloween

An alert advertising staff will find many chances to sell extra space in special events—local, national, and in school. These are only a few examples of enterprise selling. Consult the special-events calendar in the Appendix for many more special selling opportunities.

Fig. 36f below

Junior prom

Fig. 36g right

Formal social event

and electric-power advertising are examples. (See Figs. 30-36g.) Advertising can best serve all concerned by being truthful. Exaggeration, deception, omission, evasion, distortion of fact, or misleading implication are dishonest and have no place in advertising.

Chapter 3

KNOWLEDGE OF RETAIL MARKETING
IS ESSENTIAL TO SUCCESSFUL ADVERTISING

THE ADVERTISING SALESMAN SHOULD KNOW
HIS PUBLICATION'S READERS

Success in advertising salesmanship rests on knowledge of the retailing process and of the market. The former is the technique of merchandising; the latter is the composition and disposition of the buying and selling groups: the student body audience and the business community.

Knowledge of the audience is of first importance; it is the source of information that the prospective advertiser needs immediately in order to make an advertising decision.

What are the current fads in dress, coiffures, haircuts, jewelry, reading, entertainment, food? What social, academic, or athletic events will require or stimulate purchases? A formal junior prom, for instance, will lead to rentals and sales of formal dress, new hairdos and haircuts, sales of cosmetics, jewelry, corsages and boutonnieres, and perhaps taxi service.

Student buying habits should be observed. When do they shop—during lunch periods, on week ends, or after school? How many have charge accounts? How many have before- or after-school jobs? How much is the average weekly or monthly allowance or expendable income? How many read the publication for which the advertising is being solicited?

The potential advertiser wants these facts. Knowing them, he is a very likely prospect; otherwise, he is apathetic or will not advertise at all.

The publication that wants to profit from advertising will provide its prospects with an analysis of its readers' buying habits. One of the better ways to do this is to conduct a questionnaire survey every year to keep abreast of a fast-changing economy. (See Appendix B on page 159 for sample questionnaire and instructions for distribution, collection, and tabulation of results.)

The sales presentation is strengthened by use of information obtained from the survey in comparison with the figures in the American Newspaper Publishers Association Bureau of Advertising national survey "Tell It to the Teens." (See Appendix C, page 165.)

The composition and disposition of the business community as revealed by the prospect list and geography of the sales territory should be thoroughly familiar to the ad staff. In addition, alert salespeople will take full advantage of such seasonal merchandising events as Christmas, Easter, Mother's Day, Father's Day, St. Valentine's Day and Hallowe'en, and such local co-operative selling events as Dollar Days and the like. (See Appendices D-1 and D-2 for lists of likely prospects for school publications and a list of year-round selling opportunities.)

ADVERTISING SALESMAN SHOULD KNOW
THE PRINCIPLES OF RETAILING

In order to produce advertising beneficial to all concerned— reader, advertiser, publication—the solicitor should also become familiar with basic principles of retailing and what these require of advertising. Fundamental to this understanding is the tenet that advertising is only one tool of the marketing process and must be employed with comprehension of its role in relation to the several other tools. (See Appendix E.)

For example, increasing sales is only one of a complex of reasons for the use of advertising:

(1) Development of store reputation
(2) Attraction of more customers
(3) Immediate sales
(4) Increase of net profit
     (a) By reduction of sales cost
     (b) By increase of sales
(5) Stabilization of store volume

Retail advertising is called upon to perform manifold tasks, and most of these revolve around special problems. The purposes listed above lead into a field of discussion that can become too sophisticated for our present intention, but a careful look at the framework is necessary for comprehension.

First of all, a retailer must "buy" customers. Not enough people know where his store is situated, what it carries, or when, how, and for how much he sells his merchandise or service. Therefore, he must take his store to the people. He does this by advertising. But why? What about all those students and others who pass his store every day or hear about it in roundabout ways?

Well, for one thing, those passersby are not all prospects for his goods or services, and for another, not enough prospects pass the store or hear about it. Only a small proportion of a store's potential customers ever come near it in the normal course of their activities.

Consequently, the first thing a retailer must do is attract a clientele. He attempts to do this in many ways—publication advertising, store signs, window displays, radio announcements, direct mail, television, billboards, motion picture film.

A basic similarity exists in the advertising problems of all retail businesses. They must impress on the public the differences and samenesses, excellences, and advantages of buying from the particular business being advertised.

In order to accomplish this, there must be clear definition of the firm's objective. Its policy, class of customers sought, types of merchandise and services offered, and kind of advertising to be done must be specific and known.

By policy is meant the rules by which the business handles such matters as credit, discounts, check cashing, store hours, merchandise exchange, guarantees, refunds, mail orders, wrapping, and such details.

Every store is typed as to merchandise and service. Even in such a general category as men's wear, classifications range from jeans to tuxedoes and extend horizontally to include shops specializing in shoes, ties, hats, shirts, trousers, and the like.

The kind of advertising to be done is of paramount importance and not always easily decided. Not only must the choice of media conform to the store's purposes, but so must the physical construction of the advertising itself.

ONLY THE BEST IS GOOD ENOUGH

Much advertising is wasted—offering the wrong items at the wrong prices at the wrong times, in layouts and copy that fail to catch and hold attention and do the selling they are supposed to do.

In the creation of an efficient advertisement, then, only attention-compelling layouts and sales-drawing copy will suffice.

The efficiency of even the best-designed and -written advertising is limited. It cannot sell unwanted goods, services, or ideas; it must have full store cooperation; and it must be used continuously.

Numerous studies have proved that prospective customers are not an audience but a parade, the composition and tempo and direction of which are constantly changing. Of any given publication's readers, only a portion peruse all of each issue; a continuum of publication is necessary to span the entire spectrum of readership. Therefore, frequent and continuous appearance of advertising is prerequisite to its optimal efficiency.

This idea should not seem strange. A door-to-door or person-to-person selling effort would have little result if the salesperson made only two or three calls and then quit for the day. Some salesmen are so expert that they can do this and still prosper. By the same token, some ads are extraordinarily resultful. However, both would do better by extension of effort, the salesman by more presentations and the ad by more appearances.

Which is simply to say that advertising is selling.

ADVERTISING MUST SERVE THE CUSTOMER

Advertising must serve the customer or be sterile. In this regard it has a number of jobs to do in order to be influential.

First, it must be informative. It must tell the prospective customer what he should know to enable him to reach a buying decision.

The attributes of the merchandise or service must approximate the requirements of the prospect if he is to be happy with his purchase. The more closely these two sets of specifications match, the more ideal the transaction. The more transactions of this kind the store makes, the more successful it will be, other things being equal (which they never are!). In any case, it is the job of advertising to aim for this ideal customer-store relationship.

Second, advertising has the responsibility of attesting to quality of goods and services. People often say "It's a good product—you see it advertised everywhere." The feeling is general that the retailer will not unqualifiedly advertise an inferior product or service, one that he will not "stand behind," and this is true of successful advertisers. It is a serious thing to go on public record; the very fact of doing so imposes an obligation of integrity on the retailer. He responds to this situation by putting his best foot forward, and as a result the quality of advertised products is above the store norm. The forces of competition ("So you won't refund my money, eh? Okay, I'll buy elsewhere in the future!") meet and combine with those of the going-on-record process ("It says right here in the ad, etc., etc.").

The result is that the quality of advertised products and services is generally higher than that of the nonadvertised and they are more fairly priced.

Chapter 4

FOR BETTER SELLING, PLAN
THE WORK, THEN WORK THE PLAN

THREE-IN-ONE PROSPECT LIST IS A MUST

The first step in the advertising sales and production process is to establish a prospect file. To do this, make an alphabetized master list on 3 x 5 cards of all business firms that deal in products that student readers want and can buy. Sources include former advertisers as revealed by back issues of school papers, yearbooks, magazines, directories, programs, local newspapers, shopping news, buyer guides, telephone books, and the like. (See Appendix E for list of likely prospects.) Put the signature of the firm, address, phone number, and name of the advertising buyer, if known, in the upper left corner of the card.

Next, make another list, this time by *product* or *service*. Put this information first in the upper left corner of the card, then the name of firm and such, as on the other cards, and file alphabetically in a case.

Finally, make a third list, this time by *street and number,* and file according to whatever plan is most appropriate for the layout of your town or business district.

With these three cases of files completed, "beats" or sales territories can be established. (See Figs. 37, 38, 39.)

One way is simply to divide the territory geographically among the staff members.

Another is to apportion by product classification.

However this is done, either a list of accounts or another set of cards should be issued to the salesperson—not cards from the master

47

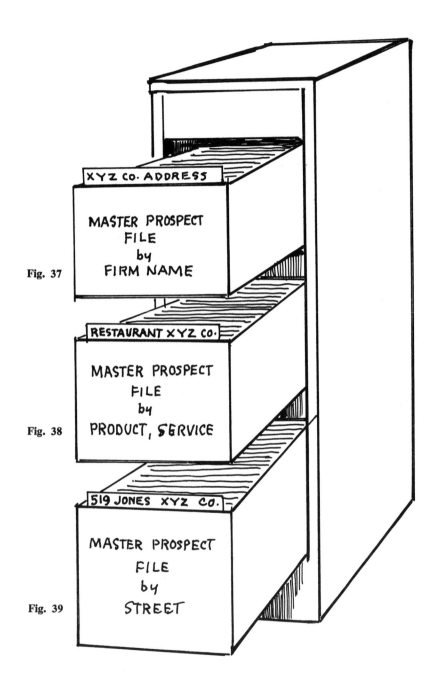

Fig. 37

XYZ CO. ADDRESS

MASTER PROSPECT FILE by FIRM NAME

Fig. 38

RESTAURANT XYZ CO.

MASTER PROSPECT FILE by PRODUCT, SERVICE

Fig. 39

519 JONES XYZ CO.

MASTER PROSPECT FILE by STREET

files, however. These should never leave their cases except for reference, and then they should be immediately replaced.

Either a carbon copy or an extra set of cards of each beat should be retained by the advertising manager, who will soon learn that staffers are forever losing theirs or leaving them at home or in their lockers.

An extra aid the writer has found invaluable is a large wall map of the sales territory, showing exact street locations of all prospects, bus lines, distances, walking or transportation times, and the like.

A little time spent by the staffers at the outset in familiarizing themselves with this map will save much time later on.

SPACE RATES: SINGLE PRICE OR SLIDING SCALE?

Space in newspapers traditionally is sold by the column inch locally, by the agate line nationally, and by page segment in yearbooks, programs, and such.

A column inch is one inch deep on the column regardless of the width, because columns vary in width. In the case of newspapers, the basic space unit should equate with the agate line, which is the basic unit of measurement in advertising placed by advertising agencies.

Fourteen agate lines equal one inch. Therefore, if the rate is to be $1 per inch, divide by 14 to get the line rate, which will be 7.142¢. This is an awkward figure. It would be better (and make agencies and school auditors happier) to set the rate at 98¢ (7¢ x 14) or $1.05 (7.5¢ x 14) per inch.

There are two schools of thought about space rates. Some publishers say the fairest system is one rate for all, arguing that this does not place the smaller business at a disadvantage as do rates based on volume or frequency. Others, and they are in the majority, favor sliding-scale schedules that offer lower rates for larger space, more frequent insertions, repetition of ads, or combinations of these factors. They assert that larger space is easier and more economical to handle and therefore merits a reduced price. They also say that the sliding-scale schedule is a selling aid.

Whatever the rate, it should be sufficient for a substantial profit. The best formula to assure this is one whose primary base is costs of production and whose secondary base is circulation.

Here is an effective formula for determining space rates:

Assumptions	Number of issues planned	XXXX
	Printing costs per issue	XXXXXX
	Other costs	XXXXX
	Total costs	XXXXXX
	Size of paper	XXXXX
	Columns per page	XXXXXX
	Inches of type per page	XXXXX
	Total inches	XXXXX
	Number of subscribers	XXXXXX
	Subscription rate	XXX
	Total circulation income	XXXXXX
	Or: Subsidy revenue	XXXXXX
	Space for advertisements	XXX%

Procedures

(1) Deduct subscription or subsidy total from total costs. Result will be amount of revenue that must come from advertising sales.

(2) Multiply inches per issue by % of advertising desired for space in each issue for ads.

(3) Then multiply this sum by the number of issues to be printed for total space for ads for the publication period.

(4) Now divide the revenue required (1) by the number of inches to be sold (2) for the average rate per inch to be charged. Inasmuch as the sales goal may not be realized or some other unforeseen problem, such as increased printing costs, may arise, it is wise to raise this rate arbitrarily by about 10%. Then either charge everyone this rate or devise a sliding scale (bulk-rate schedule) that will provide it.

The highest rate and the lowest rate on a sliding-scale rate card and the one rate on a single rate card are both unrealistic if at odds with the auditor's report.

For example, what is the *real* rate on a card that scales down from $1.50 to 75¢ an inch, or from $50 a page to $15 a quarter-page?

Only experience will tell. In case of the newspaper, the figure will be revealed by dividing the amount of money received by the number of inches printed.

For example: Number of inches 1964   1,016″
               Income received $ 965
               Average rate realized   95¢ an inch.

$$1016 \overline{)965.00}(94+$$
$$\underline{9144}$$
$$5060$$
$$4064$$

Had the guess been that a rate of $1.12 per inch (derived by adding the above-mentioned $1.50 top and 75¢ bottom rates and dividing by two) would be average, and had expenditures been based on it, the result could have been disastrous.

For instance, had the goal been a break-even based on the supposed $1.12 average, a loss of $172.92 would have been the result.

$$1016 \times 1.12 = 1137.92$$
$$1016 \times .95 = 965.00$$
$$\overline{172.92}$$

In case of the yearbook, the average rate can be figured as sales are made, and the size of the book adjusted accordingly. A good rule-of-thumb formula for establishing the rate is this:

Printing 1,000 books, 120 pages each, @ $3 $3,000
Revenue @ 1.50 each   <u>1,500</u>
                                       1,500
          Plus 25% profit   <u>375</u>
         ADVERTISING TO BE SOLD $1,875

If 25 per cent advertising is the goal, 30 pages at $62.50 per page will be required to make $1,875.

For many reasons, rate schedules as used in these examples may not produce according to expectation. A disproportionate number of the ads may be low-rate, or some advertisers may fail to pay because of a publisher's error or failure of the business. In any event, the 95¢ rate in the foregoing example is not sufficient for a profit. The margin of profit must be provided for by charging more, by the sale of more high-rate ads, by avoidance of sales to financially unstable firms, by adoption of a cash-with-copy policy, or by greater care in ad production and insertion to insure payment for all advertising published.

PRINTED FORMS MAKE THE JOB EASIER

The advertising practitioner functions more efficiently when he uses printed forms that reflect his methods and conform to standards of accurate accounting procedures. The advertising department is one of four which must correlate well. Verbal communication with the editorial or mechanical divisions seems never to work out in a student publication any better than in the professional one. "Let's have that in writing" is one of the commonest remarks in the publishing world.

RATE CARD

Heading up the list of forms is the rate card. There should be one for off-campus and another for on-campus, distinguished in some way, such as color of ink or stock.

These should be used liberally. Each prospect should receive one. Ad staffers should carry a supply on all solicitation trips. A good rate card is an excellent advertisement in itself for the publication it represents.

The card should be a complete, self-explanatory summary of all information required by the advertiser. One side should contain the rate schedule and the other related data and instructions. (See Figs. 40 and 41.)

SPACE CONTRACT

Another essential tool of the efficient advertising department is the space contract. Its use, which should be mandatory, will avoid misunderstandings that inevitably result from verbal agreements. The form should be used even in telephone and mail transactions. In

BERKELEY DAILY JACKET

OFFICIAL NEWSPAPER FOR BERKELEY HIGH SCHOOL

Milvia and Kittredge Sts., Berkeley, California
Publication Office: Room G110A   Phone TH 1-1422, Ext. 370

ADVERTISING RATE (Effective September, 1964)

National rate (Agency discount allowed) ....Col. In. 1.40

Frequency rate (same ad repeated, no copy change) ......Col. In. .85

Monthly rate, change of copy:
  1-22 column inches ....Col. In. 1.15
  23-44 column inches ....Col. In. 1.00
  45-66 column inches ....Col. In. .90
  more than 66 column inches ....Col. In. .85

Fig. 40

The Jacket is distributed every morning during second period which is extended five minutes for the purpose of reading it.

1. Deadline: Three days prior to publication.

2. Only copy suitable for reading of minors accepted.

3. No special positions promised.

4. Mechanical requirements.
   a. Column width 2 inches, depth of page 11 inches.
   b. Four columns to page.
   c. Full page 44 column inches.
   d. Can use mats but prefer original art or glossy prints as
      The Jacket is printed by the offset method.

Fig. 41

these cases the salesperson should fill in the form, including the name of the person authorizing the advertising, sign it, attach the original to the copy to be turned over to the advertising manager, and mail the duplicate to the client.

Every solicited or office sale should be recorded in a contract, signed by the salesperson and the client. Should it be overlooked, the salesperson should go to the client at the first opportunity and complete the transaction. An original order should be on file for every ad published.

The most convenient size for these contracts is 3″ x 5″, for a number of reasons:

(1) Girls like to carry their gear in handbags and boys in shirt or jacket pockets, and 3 x 5 fits comfortably into these repositories.

(2) This size is convenient for filing in the master card file, either separately or behind the prospect card.

(3) The size is handy for depositing in the merchant's cash register.

The forms should be stapled or bound into books of 25 and perforated for easy removal. (See Fig. 42.)

Some printing shops and the accounting systems of some advertising departments require no more information than that always contained in the upper left corner of the copy and layout sheets, to wit:

Bill Johnson
3x5
Name of publication
Date of insertion

But many operations need more data than this. The insertion order shown in Fig. 43, 4″ x 6″ in size, in duplicate (original and copy on different color paper), bound in pad at top, may be used as is or adapted. The original is to be pasted to the top of the ad layout sheet, and the carbon retained by the advertising manager for record-keeping and dummying purposes. It is a good idea to keep them on file until the publication period is over.

ADVERTISING ORDER

BERKELEY HIGH SCHOOL DAILY JACKET
Official School Newspaper

Date...

We, the undersigned, hereby order advertising space in the DAILY JACKET as follows:

No. Col. Inches .... Shape ....

Dates of insertion ....

Rate per inch .... Total $ ....

.... Firm ....

Jacket representative

Address ....

By ....

F124 1M 4-64

Fig. 42

ADVERTISING
INSERTION ORDER
XYZ SCHOOL NEWS

Dates to run ....

Size ....
         col. inches   shape

Position ....
               to come

Copy herewith ....

From Where? ....

When? ....

Kill ☐   **Hold** ☐

Remarks

....

....

....

By ....

Fig. 43

THE MORE SALESPEOPLE THE BETTER

The ideal learning situation is provided by alternation or rotation of staff jobs so that eventually everyone tries his hand at every job. It is utopian to suppose that this can be done in all cases, but at least the reporters and ad staff can be alternated. This avoids overspecialization to some extent and provides for coverage of more beats, especially those for which every-other-week assignments will suffice.

FIG. 44

PUBLICATION LETTERHEAD

Salutation:

　　(Number) students and adult personnel of XYZ High (College) read the XYZ News every (day, week, fortnight), and they read it thoroughly because it deals with events and ideas in which they are intimately involved.

　　They read the ads as well as the news because they have money to spend for the things they want.

　　A good way to get them to want what you have for sale is to advertise consistently in the XYZ News. The cost is small --the result in sales and good will is great.

　　Please listen when our journalism student salesman comes to see you. The story he has to tell is full of profit potential for you. Or we will be glad to take your ad by phone. Our number is _____.

　　　　　　Sincerely,

PROMOTION SMOOTHS THE WAY

No salesperson should have to make a "cold" call. Every prospect on the list should be aware not only of the existence of the publication, but also of its advantages for him. A simple mailer should be distributed at the beginning of each publication period to all prospective advertisers. Better is a letter signed by the advertising manager; it will be more personal and will say more. (See Fig. 44.)

Chapter 5

HOW TO SELL ENOUGH ADVERTISING
TO MAKE THE PUBLICATION PROFITABLE

THE BEST SOLICITATION IS INFORMATIONAL

The salesperson should be no less familiar with the facts about his publication than with those of the retail process and market disposition.

How many copies are printed? When and to whom are they distributed? What is the page size? Is the space sold by the inch or by page segment? What is the printing method—letterpress or offset? (This makes a big difference, because in the latter case mats and cuts are not necessary—only proofs and original art.) What are layout, copy, and art deadlines? What are the rates? Discounts, if any? Method of billing? Mechanical requirements? From what clients, if any, is cash with copy required?

The best solicitation is informational; therefore, a Who, What, When, Where, Why, and How summary of the foregoing makes an ideal sales talk. The time to become persuasive is after interest has been aroused.

This technique, which essentially involves the salesperson's saying who he is, what he has to offer, and why it will benefit the prospect, is classically simple and tremendously effective:

(1) Salesperson enters store and asks for advertising manager.
(2) If advertising buyer is not available, salesperson should find out when he will be and make a note to call back at that time. He does not refer to the nature of his call unless requested to do so.

(3) When confronted by the person he has asked for, salesperson introduces himself by name, school, and publication.

(4) He explains his mission: He is selling advertising for (publication). If prospect is a former advertiser, he should be thanked for previous orders and then asked for new advertising.

The salesperson should be confident, but not cocky. If the prospect is not a regular advertiser, he should be told all about the publication and given reasons why advertising in it will benefit him. He should be given a copy or a dummy of the publication or a suggested ad to examine while the salesperson is talking.

The sales talk should be solidly based on four characteristics of student buyers: (a) They have money to spend, (b) they influence the spending of their parents' money, (c) they respond readily to sales messages directed to them, and (d) they are future customers whose allegiances persist into adulthood.

This is important: In all cases the prospect should be told all he will patiently hear before being asked for the ad. The more he knows, the better he can decide and the more apt he is to decide in the solicitor's favor; and only the solicitor can tell him what he needs to know when he needs to know it. Then, and only then, should the prospect be asked to buy.

This done, a friend, as well as a sale, will have been made. In the long run the former is as important as the latter.

(5) If the prospect says he will buy an ad, no more should be said. A contract specifying size, shape, insertion dates, and rate should be immediately filled out and signed and a duplicate given to the customer.

(6) The salesperson should then obtain copy for the ad, taking careful notes and being sure to get price, sizes, quantities— the more details the better. He may not need it all, but too much is better than not enough. He should be sure to obtain everything necessary for the complete ad—copy, mats, proofs, cuts—and to establish whether a proof is to be submitted before publication or whether the publication is authorized to read proof.

(7) Finally, the solicitor should thank the client and depart. He

has other prospects to see, and his client has his work to resume.

Let us now recapitulate the mechanics of the process: All solicitors should go out on their beats prepared. They should take: (1) copies of the most recent issue of the publication, (2) copy of prospect's most recent ad, one appropriate to the occasion, or suggested layout and copy of an ad suitable for the client, (3) rate cards, (4) contract blanks, and (5) pencil and paper.

Use of these tools makes the transaction more concrete, gives the prospect some idea of what to expect, holds his attention while the salesperson explains his proposition, and helps the salesperson avoid that deadly, nonproductive approach: "Would you be interested in running an ad in (publication)?" How can he be, if he knows nothing about it?

SALES CONFERENCES INCREASE EFFICIENCY

From time to time the staff should meet to settle differences, solve problems, and plan ahead. By following the admonition of the old adage "The time to set sail is when you feel the breeze," concerted action can be taken to capitalize on coming events. For example, calls for Christmas advertising should be started in late October, and the advertising should begin to appear about Thanksgiving. Similarly, Easter advertising should be sold beginning at least a month before Easter week. This means that special-event advertising calls must be made concurrently with regular solicitations. It also highlights another truism—"Something is selling all the time"—which means that the salesperson should be aware of all campus selling opportunities— social and athletic events, scholastic programs, and the like.

Certain facts about each prospective advertiser should be known by the sales staff. Has he advertised in this or any other school publication before? How, when? How good is his credit? Has there ever been a misunderstanding with him? Who in his organization handles the advertising? When should advertising sales calls be made: day of week, time of day? Does he prefer a "suggested ad" presentation? Does he demand to see proof before publication? How many tearsheets does he want and when? Which of his ads are co-operative (see Appendix F), requiring that duplicate or triplicate memo bills with three tearsheets be sent monthly in addition to the regular billing? Has he special preferences such as for billing, ad position, ad style? Will he place advertising by phone? If he has signed a contract, what are the conditions and rate? All this information ought to be a matter of record. It should be obligatory for each salesman to learn it and enter it on the master card of each account as calls are made, or include it in a report to the advertising manager, who will enter it on the card. The salesperson should also enter it on his own prospect card for ready reference.

Only when equipped with this information about his prospective client, the retail situation in which the prospect is involved, the purchasing power and buying habits of his publication's readers, and policy details of his publication, is the salesperson ready to leave the office for his sales beat.

A glance at his relative performance standing on the sales chart on wall or blackboard may also be salutary. This device, which may be in any form, is a most effective incentive toward increased sales. One form is a drawing of a large thermometer to show total sales and a small one for each salesperson to show sales by the day, week, or month. Another that tells the story quickly is a block for each inch or unit of space sold placed after the name of each staff member. By listing the entire staff, each will feel that he has a responsibility and that the burden should not fall entirely on the advertising division. Even the editors may be sparked into bringing in some business.

The sales conferences should also include techniques for follow-up or "account servicing," of which more will be said later in this chapter.

All this requires much planning by the ad manager and staff. It is here that the admonition "Plan the work, and work the plan" applies so well.

Do It All with One Call

Out of such planning inevitably will come a strengthened conviction that selling multiple insertions is one of the best ways of increasing advertising revenue with the least effort. If you can stand one more bromide, hark to this one: "Do it all with one call." This means selling more than one insertion at a time. Most institutional advertising, such as bank, barbershop, restaurant, and service station lends itself to this.

A good way to sell multiple insertions is to suggest a schedule of once or several times a week in case of a daily, once a week in a weekly, or several scattered positions in a yearbook. Copy and layout should be different for each insertion, with a basic similarity of layout so that a continuum of impression is maintained; or two or three ads may be alternated. This places a responsibility on the staffer to change copy according to agreement. It is, however, a most efficient way to maintain a high lineage figure, as the staffer is relieved of so many sales calls and gains time for copy writing or calling on other accounts.

Some ways to vary the ads according to such a technique are: (1) same size, (2) alternate big and small, (3) big and smaller, and (4) small to big (Rolling Thunder). (See Figs. 45-49.)

Frequencies to suggest will vary from business to business. Periods to suggest range all the way from one month to the entire publishing period. The important thing is to suggest the multiple insertions. The businessman is aware of their advisability, but the salesman must take the initiative and be willing to follow through on the transaction. However the strategy is applied, it pays off in greater space sales and more satisfied advertisers.

"Follow-Up" Should Follow "Follow-Through"

Here are four things to do that will make friends, influence people, and help sell more advertising:

(1) Arrange for proofs to be read by the publication staff, with the understanding that in event of error a corrected republication will serve as a billable make-good. Running proofs to advertisers should be avoided—staffs just don't have the time. If the advertiser insists, set deadlines for such copy well in advance of publication date.

(2) Mail or personally deliver three copies of the newspaper and one of the yearbook to each advertiser immediately on publication of the ad. Be sure to mark the ad. (See Fig. 49a.)

(3) Write a letter of thanks to each advertiser at the end of each publishing period.

(4) Keep several files of the publication on hand for clipping and reference.

Fig. 45 Same size

Fig. 46 Alternate—big and small

Fig. 47 Big and smaller

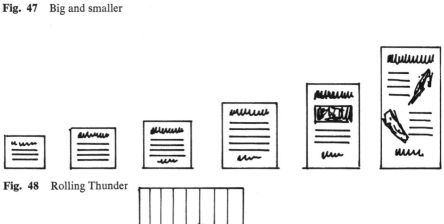

Fig. 48 Rolling Thunder

Fig. 49

Crusty Fish Sticks
With Tartar Sauce
Buttered W.K. Corn
Under-The-Sea Salad
Chocolate Pudding
Third Quart Milk

BLOW-OUT BOX

Dear Blow-Out Box;

During the past few weeks I have been unable to understand the repeated grumbles from students who feel that the Jacket is disappointing. Despite the fact that there are numerous mistakes and occasional insufficient coverage, I've felt that because the Jacket is our newspaper, published daily, and free, why complain? But now I see it and feel it too; I would rather see no Jacket than a newspaper whose staff appears to have its finger in its ear. For instance, the edition of Thursday, April 13. There's an article I wrote for the benefit of kids who wish to run for cheerleader for next year. The article printed contains misleading information, contrary to the clear instructions I wrote in the original. Why can't you print the stated facts instead of getting your "creative" and confused mind's work in there? Another thing, people at BHS complain about lack of school spirit; well, how can there be very much when the Jacket staff, those who should find out the facts and inform others of it, doesn't even know that Patty Schantz is a pompon girl, not a cheerleader? Really, this is getting ridiculous! Just because the end of the year is near doesn't mean you can be on your bottom instead of your toes. So come on, Staff; you may be No. 1, but believe me, you do need to try harder. And please, print this letter as it is! !
Karin Hern

Dear Blow-Out Box

In a letter to the Jacket on Wed., April 12, a student complained about the tracking system at Berkeley High and how it was causing racial segregation. If it is causing racial segregation, is it the fault of the system itself? In the first place I would like to point out that the educational system in our country was not developed for the purpose of integration, but for education. Secondly, the tracking system was not devised to segregate the races, but to segregate different levels of achievement In the tracking system, a person is placed in a class equal to his level of achievement. A person with a low level of achievement will be put in a low level class; a person with a high level will be put in a high level class. Once a student is placed in a track doesn't mean he is bound to that track. He can move up if he is willing to make the effort. I don't feel the tracking system is at fault. It seems to me that some people are just using it as a scapegoat.
Allen Goetzel
Dick Bruce

Dear Little Blow-Out Box,

Although I fully support Zede Avi and Schmeg's right to free speech and do not believe that their "Waves" joke of April 12 was in poor taste, these two "witty gentlemen" did appear rather snobbish in their "allusion to the late Vincent Van Gogh". Or, maybe I am just too naive to appreciate good humor —if so, please excuse me.
Tina Delgado

Fig. 49a

Chapter 6

THE DUMMY BRINGS BUYER
AND SELLER TOGETHER

DETERMINE A PROFITABLE PROPORTION

The distribution of advertising and editorial content in newspapers, magazines, and yearbooks is of significance to several participants in the publishing process. The editor's interest is aesthetic. The advertiser wants maximum readership of his message. The business manager wants the publication to be profitable, or at least break even. The printer's abiding concern is ease of production.

The first step in this "dummying" process is determination of a desirable proportion of advertising to editorial content. In most schools this ranges between 25 per cent in yearbooks and 40 per cent in newspapers. The percentage will depend on advertising rate, costs of production, and desired profit.

A dependable formula for such a percentage is:

Costs of production	XXXXXXXXXXXX
minus circulation income	XXXXXXXXXX
equals advertising revenue needed	XXXXXX
divided by average space rate	XXX
equals amount of space to be sold	XXXXX
divided by space available	XXXX
equals percentage of space for advertising	XX

Adherence to formula is easier in the case of the yearbook or other infrequent publications, as there is time before final deadline to ad-

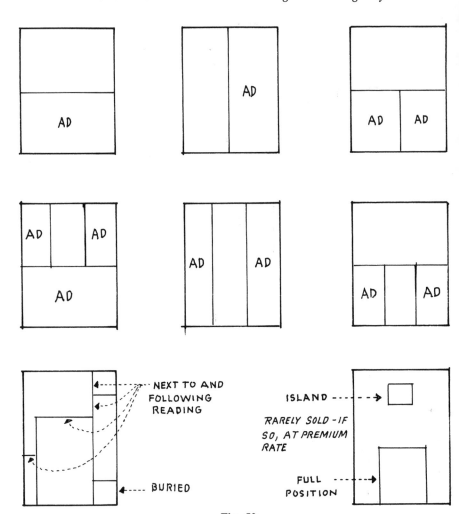

Fig. 50

just size to conform with advertising sales. But the hectic, crowded schedule of the newspaper does not permit of such flexibility. One issue may contain 10 per cent advertising, another 70 per cent, still another 40 per cent. In addition, there are seasonal fluctuations such as Hallowe'en, Easter, Christmas, and campus events.

Besides this variation in total volume, advertising itself is varied and unpredictable as to size and shape. Ad layouts are almost always unchangeable because of illustration and type specifications, and the advertiser has the final say on the size and shape of his advertisement, modified only by policies of the publication. (See Fig. 50.)

The editor and advertising manager should therefore co-operate closely on dummy policy, and the advertising manager should have the final say because he has far less control over advertising than the editor has over straight matter.

ADS SHOULD BE INTEGRATED WITH READING MATTER

Inasmuch as the advertiser is buying readership (which is all, except its physical self, that the publication has for sale), advertising should be integrated with editorial content to the mutual benefit of all concerned. Newspaper readership is of shorter duration than that of less frequently issued publications such as yearbooks. Knowing this, wise advertisers schedule their ads consistently over periods of time —the oftener the better—in order to maximize readership. Each appearance of the message attracts a portion of the paper's total readership, and this attention accumulates in ratio to the number of appearances.

Each ad, therefore, should be so dummied that it will have the best chance of being read; that is, it should be placed as close to reading matter as possible. The final result of good dummying should be a pleasing, effective integration of advertising and editorial matter. (See Fig. 51.)

Achievement of such a happy mutuality is easier if the editor delays the styling of editorial matter until the dummy has been received from the advertising department. It should not be supposed that this is the end of the matter, however. Often the advertising manager can rearrange the dummy to meet, or at least compromise with, the needs of the editorial department; and he should do so whenever possible.

STYLING TO PREVENT BURYING ADS

The style of the ad dummy is predicated on several considerations: maximum readership for each ad, advertiser preference, and mechanical requirements. The best styles for these purposes are (1) to the left, (2) to the right, and (3) valley. (See Fig. 51a.) Research shows no appreciable difference in readership, but advertisers like the right-hand position best. Other position requests by advertisers, in order

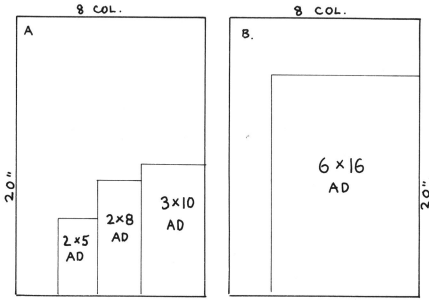

Fig. 51

Two pages are available. To be dummied are: 2 x 5, 2 x 8, 3 x 10, 6 x 16. Obviously, the 3 x 10 and 6 x 16 must be placed on separate pages. Either of the two-column ads may be dummied on page B, and either or both atop the 3 x 10 on page A, but that exhausts the possibilities. Dummying both two-column ads on page B would result in one being "buried," an undesirable and unnecessary situation.

of preference, are: (newspaper) front page, third page, back page, facing center pages, special pages according to the nature of the advertising (such as sports, society, financial), following reading, next to reading, full position, island, and bottom; (yearbook, magazine, etc.) outside front page, inside front page, outside back page, inside back page, page facing inside back, facing center pages, full position, next to reading, following reading, island, and bottom.

Nearly all publications charge extra for guaranteed position. Great care should be exercised in granting special positions to avoid promising the same spot to more than one client. This is almost sure to happen when several salespeople are soliciting at the same time. A way around this problem is to call on the most likely prospects for the premium positions first, obtaining permission to dummy in alternative positions or on alternative days. A definite promise should never

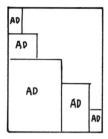 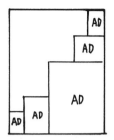 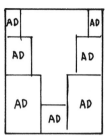

Fig. 51a

be made. The right of final decision should always be reserved for the advertising manager.

THERE'S MORE TO DUMMYING THAN MEETS THE EYE

One of the major weaknesses of scholastic publishing is dummying for the eye only—the prejudiced or unpracticed eye of the editor or adviser who for one reason or another scorns advertising and segregates it in special sections or pages, usually at the end of the publication.

This approach is indefensible if the object of soliciting advertising is a profitable publication. The advertiser is purchasing maximum readership of his message with due regard for the price he pays for its publication. He is not so naive as to believe this message will be sought out for its own sake. He expects his space to be next to or following editorial content.

Businessmen often complain that school publications hold them in contempt even while seeking their support. Advertisers come to this conclusion because scholastic journalists make little or no attempt to help make advertising pay, either by effective copy and layout or by next-to-reading positioning. Newspapers and magazines are more realistic in this regard and therefore carry the most advertising. Nearly all yearbooks, however, continue to treat their advertising clients shabbily, and their share of available advertising revenue is at a low ebb. Faced by rising printing costs and shrinking income, annuals are being discontinued at an alarming rate. This is a distinct loss to the well-being of the academic community as well as to the democratic free-enterprise economy, and it could be avoided by adopting the honorable, realistic approach of professional publishing.

In addition to the positioning of his advertising so as to guarantee fullest possible readership, the advertiser has the right to expect a high standard of excellence in the editorial content. Uninteresting, poorly written copy and badly photographed, hazily printed pictures seriously diminish advertising effectiveness. The more time and interest the reader devotes to a page, the better chance the advertiser has of being noticed and read. This is not, however, to place the entire blame for unproductive advertising on the shoulders of the student publication. The advertiser realizes that the medium is only a potential force, that the appeals and techniques of advertising itself are the most important determinants of effectiveness; in short, that he gets from his use of space only what he puts into it and that the reader must be rewarded for the time and attention he expends on it.

Yearbooks, with their more specialized reader appeal, should contain a well-balanced mix of historical, human interest, interpretative, and literary copy and illustration, so interestingly written and presented as to invite rereading.

The newspaper, whose appeal is more general, should be timely and informative.

Pictures should not be overemphasized as the key to readership in either yearbook or newspaper. Professional publishers have long known that although illustrations definitely attract readers, they do not necessarily hold them. Pictures have less readership value than text in yearbooks and magazines, according to a survey of magazines by advertising agencies.

To be effective, pictures must relate closely with text to tell a story, evoke a memory, inspire participation.

No advertiser publicity should be permitted in editorial content. Publicity is easily recognizable as advertising in disguise. Its presence destroys reader confidence, and interest in both editorial and advertising content.

In sum, while the advertiser should have no voice in the content of a publication, he does have an abiding and vested interest in its quality. He knows that interesting, enthusiastic, and accurate editorial content attracts and holds readership, and he consistently advertises with large space in publications that provide this kind of reading and whose policies permit his advertising to be closely associated with it.

To those whose policies do not permit it, he either says "No!" or doles out the smallest amount possible as a grudging donation.

Under certain circumstances it may be impossible to achieve next-

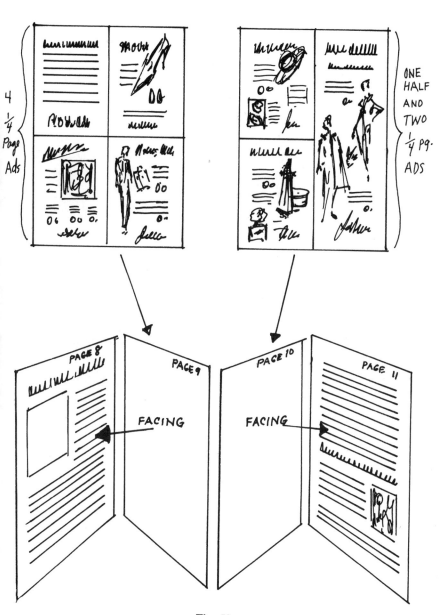

4
1/4
Page
Ads

ONE
HALF
AND
TWO
1/4 Pg.
ADS

PAGE 8

PAGE 9

PAGE 10

PAGE 11

FACING

FACING

Fig. 52

to-reading placement of advertising. For example, co-ordination of selling with editorial copy preparation may be out of the question so that the dummies of entire signatures without ads must go to the printer, and the advertisements must therefore be grouped. But they need not be segregated from the editorial content. They can be dummied by the page, back to back, and these pages can be dropped into the publication dummy anywhere so that each page of ads is faced by a page of reading matter. (See Fig. 52.) In this case extra effort by the staff will be required to compensate for the fact that the ads are somewhat on their own, with no help from immediately adjacent editorial matter. The editorial content will have to be superior and the advertising exceptionally well prepared. The layouts and copy will have to be specially attractive so as to achieve readership. There also should be a provocatively written table of contents in the front of the book calling attention to the advertising pages.

A technique that is gaining popularity with advertisers is the pictorial layout, in which students are photographed modeling clothing and demonstrating products and services. With different students in each picture and youthful copy that ties in with the spirit of the illustrations, variety and individuality are assured. Nearly every publication using this photo-text method reports more satisfied advertisers, greater revenues and net incomes, and happier readers. However, to say, or even imply, that the student models are pictured in the act of buying—unless they spontaneously are—is a violation of the "truth-in-advertising" policy so basic to successful publishing.

BOOK TWO

How to Write and Construct Advertising

Chapter 7

THE LAYOUT IS A MAP OF THE AD-TO-BE

The advertising practitioner should be reasonably skillful in lettering, measurement, proportion, and design. This makes it possible for him to judge more precisely internal distances and balances of the elements and thus create varied and interesting layouts. His finished product should be legible to the printer and attractive to the reader.

It is assumed that the student has had some drawing experience, if no more than that used in writing, but has never attempted design or draftsmanship. This does not matter. If one can write, one can letter. No matter how rough first attempts may be, time and practice will give lettering a professional touch.

The first step in practice is to copy as exactly as possible a few letters of some standard type face. (See Fig. 53.)

After this has been done several times, a line of layout lettering should be copied. Letters should be more loosely distributed than in a line of printed type. Extreme precision should not be attempted. Free and easy is the rule; otherwise the fingers will "freeze up" and the letters will be stiff and cramped. These lettering exercises should be given a good workout as a prelude to practice in making layouts. (See Fig. 54.)

Three questions immediately suggest themselves when a definition of a "layout" is requested. What is the purpose of a layout? What are the principles of its construction? How is it made?

A layout is a visualization, sketch, design, or map of the finished ad. It corresponds to a blueprint, an architect's detail drawing, or an

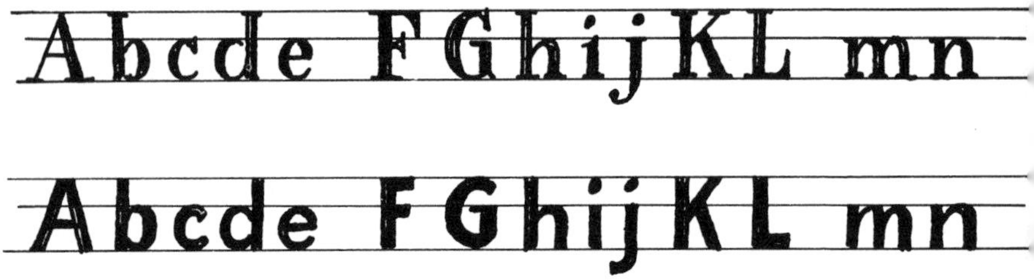

Abcde FGhijKL mn

Abcde FGhijKL mn

Fig. 53

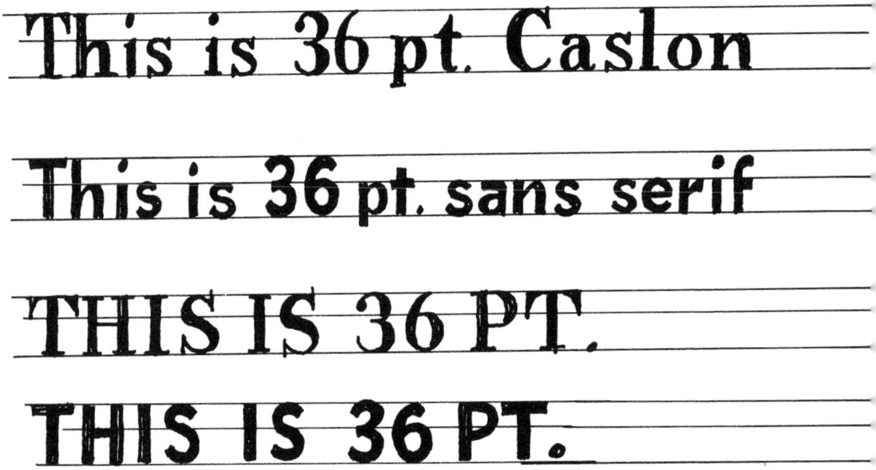

This is 36 pt. Caslon

This is 36 pt. sans serif

THIS IS 36 PT.

THIS IS 36 PT.

Fig. 54

engineering draft. It helps the ad writer style and size the elements so they will fit together into a coherent final composition.

If for no other reason, the layout is necessary as a guide for the printer, showing him how he is to set and put together the various elements.

For optimum composing-room efficiency, the ad should be sent to the print shop in two parts: the layout and copy to be hand-set on one piece of paper, and the copy to be set by machine on another.

A second purpose of the layout is for presentation to a prospective advertiser as part of the space-selling process. (See Fig. 55.)

Its most important purpose, however, is to attract the attention

Fig. 55

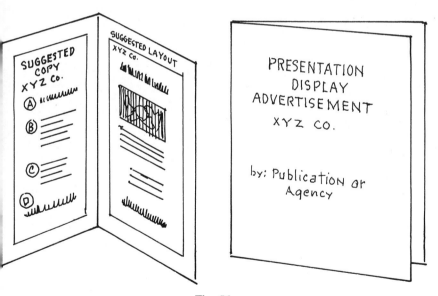

Fig. 56

A carefully prepared presentation impresses the prospect. Staple copy and layout sheets together inside a manila folder and spray with fixative so that the pencilling will not smudge. Then tape a sheet of tracing paper over one of them to keep them apart. Letter the cover appropriately.

of the reader of the publication in which it appears as a finished ad. (See Fig. 56.)

The more the layout looks like the finished, printed product, the better it has been prepared. Therefore, familiarity with the principles of layout construction is essential.

A LAYOUT HAS MANY ELEMENTS

A layout may contain any or all of these elements:

Border
Headline
Sub-headline(s)
Illustration(s)
Copy block(s)
Price(s)
Service item(s)
Signature
Address(es)
Phone number(s)

Note that the term layout means mechanical arrangement of the elements. It is to be distinguished from visualization of ideas, which will be discussed later. (See Fig. 57.)

PROCEDURE: TYPE LINES HEAVY, GUIDELINES LIGHT

Type may be shown on a layout in several ways—parallel straight lines, wavy lines, broad flat lines executed with one stroke of flattened pencil lead. Whichever is fastest is best. Speed is of the essence in advertising construction. Deadline is always near.

Some layout people, perhaps most, look upon type lines as simply indicating the tonal effects of type. This is not correct, however; they also indicate the number of lines of type in the copy block. Therefore this rule: *One type line for each line of copy.* Thus seven type lines in a copy block means that there will be seven lines of type in the finished ad. This method makes for easier type fitting.

Sometimes students ask whether the type line indicates the center of the line of type. If it did, the first line would be slightly down from the top of the space filled by the copy block and the bottom slightly up. In a sense this is logical, but for practical purposes the top line should be the top boundary and the lower line the bottom boundary

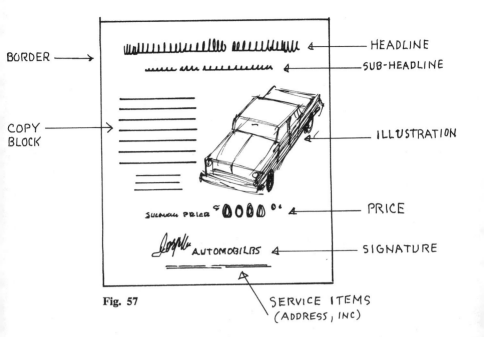

BORDER

HEADLINE

SUB-HEADLINE

COPY
BLOCK

ILLUSTRATION

PRICE

SIGNATURE

SERVICE ITEMS
(ADDRESS, INC)

Fig. 57

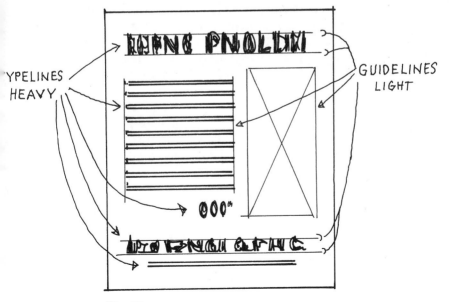

YPELINES
HEAVY

GUIDELINES
LIGHT

Fig. 58

of the copy block. Then, if there are seven lines in the copy block, there are six equal spaces between them.

Copy blocks are bounded at the left and right, and the weight of type and of the other elements are indicated by the use of guidelines. (See Fig. 58.) Notice that guidelines are much lighter than type lines. This principle can be of immense value in making layouts that look professional: TYPE LINES *HEAVY,* GUIDELINES *LIGHT.* This maxim has a practical aspect. The difference between the two kinds of lines is an aid to the printer; one glance at the layout shows what goes where and how.

The Elements Are Components of Design

The fundamentals of layout design are *Unity, Coherence, Balance, Motion,* and *Display.*

In a *unified* layout the various items are grouped according to kind or price, and all the elements are logically related to one another.

A definite, clearcut pattern characterizes the *coherent* layout. It "hangs together." The exterior margins are greater than the interior space.

Balance, or structural soundness, is achieved by symmetrical or asymmetrical (harmoniously random) arrangement of the elements.

Devices such as arrows, dots, lines, and element placement that direct or influence "gaze motion or direction" comprise the principle of *motion* (layout movement or dynamics). (See Figs. 59-66.)

All of these, plus the contrast of size, shape, tone, and color with their surroundings, produce the effect of emphasis or *display* that is the sole goal of the layout.

Simplicity is the keynote. Art and typographical services are not always available, and the printer must often make do with limited materials. Speed and economy are essential. The layout must be easy for the advertising practitioner to construct, the printer to set, and the reader to comprehend.

How well the finished product meets these principles depends on the quality and disposition of the materials of which the layout is made—the elements.

In making a layout one may assemble the elements in three ways:

(1) Draw them.

(2) Cut units from other sources and paste them into position.

Fig. 59 Unity

Fig. 60 Coherence

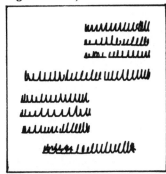

Fig. 61 Gaze motion

Fig. 62 Informal balance

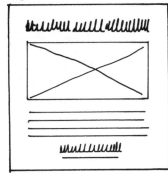

Fig. 63 Formal balance

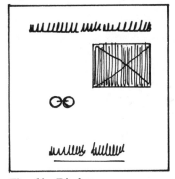

Fig. 64 Display

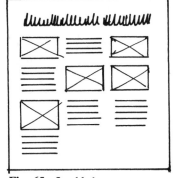

Fig. 65 Jumbled

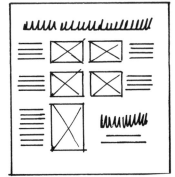

Fig. 66 Simplified

(3) Trace the various elements in proper position on a transparent overlay.

No matter which of the three methods is used, the rough or first draft should be edited for: Simplification, Eye Appeal, Focus, Visual Flow (Sequence), and Style. (See Figs. 67-71.)

SIMPLIFICATION

The impression of fewer units is created by rearranging scattered elements in the simplest possible ways, thereby making reading (and buying from) the advertisement much easier.

EYE APPEAL

Elements of the layout, individually and collectively, ought to be pleasing to the eye and easy to read. There should be an attractive relationship among the various elements.

FOCUS

The layout should attract attention to the one element or combination of elements that best conveys the message—the focal point. One of the following elements should be dominant: Price, Illustration, Headline, Copy.

VISUAL FLOW

The aim in layout construction should be the sequence of ideas and placement of the elements so as to carry the eye from one to the other in logical succession. All the principles of Balance, Coherence, Unity, Motion, Optical Center, and Display come into play in this exercise of the art.

STYLE

Store characteristics are reflected in this facet of the layout-making process. These usually fall into one of two classifications, fashion or promotion.

Advertising style should be so distinctive as to immediately identify the advertiser, and flexible enough to be applied to all kinds of advertising—from institutional to promotional. And it should be consistent—have continuity—so as to be recognizable in all types of ads used by the advertiser.

Fig. 67 Eye appeal

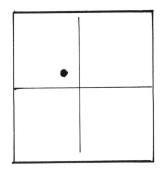

Fig. 68 Focal point

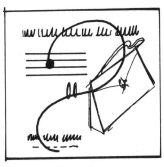

Fig. 69 Visual flow

Fig. 70 Fashion

Fig. 71 Promotion

Fig. 67 Headline should identify, dramatize illustration, and synthesize copy, which should describe illustration.

Fig. 68 Natural focal point in an area of bounded space is left and slightly above center. Dominant element should be or begin here.

Fig. 69 The eye travels from focal point to the headline, then down through illustration to signature.

Fig. 70 The accent is on style as the picture occupies the focal point. Price is played down.

Fig. 71 The accent is on volume of sales. The low price is on the focal point and emphasized by size.

Chapter 8

COPY TELLS THE READER WHAT
HE WANTS TO KNOW

The Message Is Enhanced by the Clear Statement

Expert writing, drawing on knowledge of product and market, is essential for effective advertising. The reader wants to know many facts. What does it look like? How is it made or done? What is it made of? What are its uses and benefits?

Inasmuch as advertising is selling, and selling is telling, the message is enhanced by the clear statement, which is best conveyed by simple, concise, complete copy.

It should be specific and grammatical. Sentences should be simple and complete, paragraphs short and to the point. Complex construction has no place in advertising.

The bulk of advertising copy is description and persuasion, and these are best accomplished by standard writing.

This is not to say that advertising does not permit of adroit, colorful, imaginative writing. Indeed, these are the very hallmarks of effective retail copy. However, these qualities spring from ideas, not mechanics. The simplest expression of the profound spells classicism in all the arts—of which the writing of advertising copy is one.

The aim of the advertising copy writer is a provocative, informative, influential message, and this is best achieved by basing the copy on the following key appeals:

(1) Life
(2) Love
(3) Comfort
(4) Personal importance
(5) The senses: Touch, Taste, Smell, Sight, Hearing

These appeals are fundamental and, to the extent that the merchandise or service is timely and valuable, infallible.

APPEAL DIRECTLY TO THE READER

This philosophy requires the "you" approach. To insure inclusion of the copy appeals, as well as all other essential ingredients of the selling message, prepare an outline first—and do not deviate from it. For example, here is an outline for the succeeding copy:

A. Your life and the lives of your loved ones are at stake.
   1. Do not endanger them by driving on worn, unsafe tires.
B. Buy puncture-resistant Safety-Tread tires.
   1. Let us equip your car with them now.
C. Safety-Treads' woven steel and fabric construction is patented.
   1. There are no other tires like them.
   2. Many owners report 50,000 miles without a flat.
D. Safety-Treads offer life insurance at no extra premium.
   1. They are competitively priced.
E. Let us demonstrate.
   1. Come in

"It is your life and the lives of your loved ones that are at stake," reads the copy. "Don't endanger them by driving on worn, unsafe tires. Come in today and let us equip your car with puncture-resistant Safety-Treads.

"A moment's inspection of a cut-away section of a Safety-Tread will convince you. So unique is the woven steel and fabric construction that it is protected by patent. No other tire is remotely like it.

"Many owners report that their Safety-Treads have lasted 50,000 miles without going flat. You, too, can enjoy the sense of security such performance assures.

"Here is 'life insurance' at no extra premium, as Safety-Treads are competitively priced. Come in and let us demonstrate."

All five copy appeals are utilized in the foregoing example:

Life ("Your life and the lives of")
Love ("Your loved ones")
Sense of Sight ("A moment's inspection")

Comfort ("Don't endanger"; "sense of security")
Personal importance ("You, too, can enjoy")

The copy formula is quickly apparent: Emotionalization/Rationalization. This prescription is basic to all successful selling. The "you" approach is the vehicle for customer benefit, in which the whole idea of resultful advertising copy is embodied. Why else would the prospect react to the message? Only in the most exceptional cases will he buy just to help the seller. Therefore customer benefit must be logical, timely, and the theme of the copy, beginning with the headline.

For example, the first two lines of headline for the tire copy would be:

PROTECT YOURSELF AND FAMILY FROM ACCIDENT
WITH PUNCTURE-RESISTANT SAFETY-TREAD TIRES

Secondarily, benefit to the seller is communicated by associating the product with him in the headline:

PROTECT YOURSELF AND FAMILY FROM ACCIDENT
WITH PUNCTURE-RESISTANT SAFETY-TREAD TIRES
EXCLUSIVELY IN YOUR TOWN AT XYZ TIRE CO.

Then the first paragraph of the copy, the "lead," beginning with "It is your life," immediately develops the customer-benefit theme.

QUALITY IS NOT AN APPEAL
It will be noted that except for reference to the 50,000 miles of wear, and the steel-and-fabric shield, quality is referred to only by implication. The reason for this is that quality of itself is not an appeal. It is a reason for a benefit, which is a powerful appeal.

Obviously the steel-and-fabric feature, alone and unrelated to a benefit, would be of no importance or interest to the prospective customer. The benefit that may appeal to him is the puncture-resistance, for which the steel-and-fabric construction is the reason. The other benefit is a possible 50,000 miles of puncture-less wear, the reason for which is not given in the copy. Implied is either extra-tough or extra-plentiful tread rubber in addition to the unique construction.

With the main benefit closely associated with the firm name in the headline, developed in the first paragraph, and detailed thereafter, the job is almost done. But not quite. Comes now the closing, often the most difficult part of the task.

This final paragraph should quickly sum up the reasons the reader will benefit from taking the desired action and ask him to do so.

The example copy does this. It says:

"Here is 'life insurance' at no premium, as the Safety-Tread is competitively priced. Come in and let us demonstrate."

This example represents general or institutional copy designed for the more slowly and deliberately read yearbook or magazine. It would probably appear in the newspaper in the following style, a paragraph of institutional, followed by terse, staccato specifications:

50,000 MILES WITHOUT A FLAT!

Many users of Safety-Tread Tires report more!

Don't endanger the lives of your loved ones by driving on old, worn tires—turn them in now for new Safety-Treads at XYZ Tire Co.

- Patented steel and fabric carcass
- Puncture-resistant
- Thick, long-wearing tread
- Skid-resistant tread design
- Free mounting
- Free wheel balancing
- Fast service

760 x 14 white sidewall $28.95 with trade-in. Other sizes proportionately low. 30-, 60-, 90-day charge accounts invited. Time payments to suit your budget. Open daily 6 A.M to 10 P.M.

XYZ TIRE COMPANY
1000 Broadway

COPY APPEALS VARY

Not all copy appeals are present in every ad. For example, the appeals in the following are Sense of Sight, Comfort, and Personal

Importance: "When going formal, the most important people rent from XYZ Co., because XYZ apparel makes you look important (at no extra cost)."

Sense of Taste and Life are the appeals of this one: "Nutritious quarter-pound hamburgers, dripping with flavor, 55¢ at XYZ." Love is the appeal of: "Shop XYZ for Mother's Day gifts." And so on.

COPY MUST BE COMPLETE AND SPECIFIC

All pertinent facts—sizes, colors, fabrics, styling or fashion, design, construction, special or exclusive features or uses—should be included so that the reader knows everything essential about the advertised items. Many a sale is lost because the reader assumes that the store does not have his size, or that the item costs more than he can afford. However, copy should not be hardened by inconsequential details. It should have a warm, sincere and enthusiastic tone. If the appeal is to women, feminine words should be used (dainty, thrilling, gentle); if to men, masculine ones (elegant, stirring, powerful). If the beginning is emotional ("She will just love this XYZ Vacuum Cleaner"), the ending should be reason ("It will save her hours of hard work").

High price quotations need not be avoided. Often readers will overestimate omitted prices. If the advertised price is high, however, an explanation is in order. A low price should likewise be supported by facts that engender belief and acceptance, such as closeout sale, floor sample, odd size, clearance, or special purchase.

Savings the reader makes when he buys at the advertised price, and information on credit or lay-away plans, mail or phone orders, or delivery services should be included—and always the store name, address, phone number, and hours.

The brand (if any) of the items should be specified, to capitalize on the preselling done by the manufacturer in national advertising and to enhance the retailer's reputation for quality.

Multiple sales will result from inclusion of related items in the same ad. For example, a girls' shoe ad ought to include matching gloves and handbags; a swim suit ad might offer beach robes, thongs, hats, umbrellas, and the like.

The rationalized emotion formula will result in more readable and effective copy regardless of the subject, but care must be exercised to avoid overdoing it. Readers tend to reject heavy-handed writing. Unusual or difficult words and extremes of emotion and reason must be avoided. Many people distrust the far-fetched. Others misunderstand it. The time-honored journalistic rule is a good one: Never underestimate the reader's intelligence or overestimate his vocabulary. Everybody understands simple language—nobody resents it.

COPY SHOULD BE SPECIFIC

The ad should have only one central objective, specifically stated in terms of the reader. Some of these are: (1) to obtain a large number of buyers for one product or a line of products, (2) to attract one buyer for one item, and (3) to persuade present customers to buy now for future needs.

In order to make his message more personal and specific, the copywriter should have clearly in mind the kind of people he wants to influence. He should know all the demographic details: age, sex, race, religion, social level, occupation, income, geographical distribution, education, attitudes, customs, traditions, political leanings— in other words, the composition and disposition of his audience.

Preparing an outline forces the writer to set down in advance the basic appeals, consumer benefits, product qualities, and supporting details that are the framework of the selling message.

Finally, "facts sell more." Shoppers want all the facts before buying. Therefore, copy must be specific. Excessive claims and superlatives weaken specificity and should be avoided. If price or quality is declared to be unbelievable, the reader is likely to take the ad at its word.

Self-discipline and preparation are the hallmarks of good advertising copy-writing. Close adherence to the principles of standard writing and style will help achieve "down-to-earth" copy.

Among these principles are word economy; sentence unity, variety, and simplicity; short paragraphs; appropriate transitions; strong verbs, and onomatopoeia (use of words that sound like what they mean, such as "crackle, sizzle, hiss").

Distinctive style is achieved by being natural, brief, lucid, euphonious, and vivid.

The writer who abides by these rules will become fluent. He who misuses them will become only glib.

Chapter 9

HEADLINES: CONDENSE THEM WELL
TO TELL AND SELL

THE HEADLINE: ATTENTION-GETTING DEVICE

The headline, the primary device for getting reader attention, should be "as short as possible, as long as necessary." It should be succinct and active, an accurate condensation of the story. It should attract and hold attention by its content as well as by its typography, which means that it should be written from the viewpoint of the prospective buyer, in terms of his own selfish interests. The few words in a headline have a lot of work to do, work that requires brain as well as brawn; therefore, they must be well chosen and well expressed.

Headlines fall into four general categories: Label, Informative, Provocative, Selective.

The label headline is to be avoided; it is a noncommittal tag, static and sterile, telling—and therefore selling—nothing.

The other three, however, are the stock-in-trade of the advertising copy writer, just as they are of his counterpart, the news reporter. Each has its specific purpose.

THE INFORMATIVE IS PERTINENT

Pertinent details or concepts characterize informative headlines, and they should be objective and vigorous.

For example:

MAJOR FOLKSINGERS
ON SINGLE LP
$1.98 TOMORROW ONLY AT XYZ

or

WIN FREE
RACER BICYCLE
AT XYZ CYCLERY

or

WE HOLD THE RELISH
OR SHOOT THE WORKS!
TRY OUR 19¢ BURGER

The Provocative Teases and Challenges

The provocative headline seeks to engage the attention of the reader and move him to continue reading by teasing or challenging him. The purpose of this approach is to pique the interest, arouse curiosity. It may be, and often is, oblique or peripheral, but in all cases it should derive from and specifically refer to the subject. Otherwise it may be vague, obscure, or provocative in some other context.

For example:

DON'T WORRY ABOUT THE PRICE—
IT'S FROM XYZ COMPANY
(Rest of ad—photo of girl in fur coat)

ENJOY REAL FRUIT FLAVOR!
(Rest of ad—illustration of ice cream sundae and brand)

AND MANKIND SHALL NOT DIE!
(Rest of ad—illustration and descriptive copy of book)

WOULD YOU LIKE TO EARN
$500 THIS SUMMER?
(Rest of ad—copy and illustration promoting sign-up with employment agency)

The Selective Discriminates

All retail advertising headlines are selective to some degree, be they label, informative, or provocative, because the retail appeal is always directed to some specific audience, differentiated according to age, sex, occupation, ambition, income bracket, and the like. This headline concentrates on some specific feature of merchandise or service, or customer whim or need.

For example:

(1) IT TAKES A TOUGH SHOE
LIKE XYZ'S "MARATHON"
FOR RECORD CROSS-COUNTRY
(Directed to cross-country runners)

(2) ONE WHIFF OF EXOTICA PERFUME
WILL PUT HIM UNDER YOUR SPELL
(Directed to romantic girls)

(3) XYZ'S M-80
WILL QUICKLY END
YOUR STICKY-VALVE WOES
(Directed to car owners)

(4) THE $45 SUIT WITH THE $75 LOOK
NOW ONLY $29.50 AT XYZ
(Directed to boys from low-income families)

(5) NOW! SHEER NYLON
HOSIERY THAT WON'T
LADDER, RUN, OR STRETCH
(Directed to girls who are hard on hosiery)

The subhead should integrate closely with the top headline, revealing the how or what of the promised benefit. Nothing should be left to guesswork; yet if possible, the imagination should be titillated.

Following are suggested subheads for the foregoing headlines:

(1) Many wearers report
as much as two years'
wear per pair

(2) What's $5 per ounce
when your future's at stake?

(3) One 50¢ bottle of this potent additive
will rid your engine of ping
and increase its power

(4) One-week introductory sale only!
Every suit guaranteed
finest tailoring, fit, style

(5) Double your money back
if not as advertised

The first lines of copy must, in their turn, develop the subhead and headline:

(1) Writes champion miler Lars Frome: "After four semesters of hard use, my Marathons are still good for more. The uppers don't have a crack, the cleats are firmly attached to the tough, flexible soles."

(2) Furthermore, the flacons are so exquisitely fashioned of cut glass that they make lovely conversation pieces for your dresser.

(3) Rough, noisy performance quickly succumbs to M-80. Just put a bottleful into your tank with every gas fill and forget those pesky valves.

(4) Don't let a slim budget keep you from dressing well. XYZ suits are made from the same patterns as the most expensive custom models.

(5) These marvelous products of a revolutionary knitting process are exclusive in this city at XYZ.

Now for the completed text—tying headline, subhead, and first lines of copy together:

(1) IT TAKES A TOUGH SHOE
LIKE XYZ'S MARATHON
FOR RECORD CROSS-COUNTRY

Many wearers report
as much as two years'
wear per pair

Writes champion miler Lars Frome: "After four semesters of hard use, my Marathons are still good for more. The uppers don't have a crack, the cleats are firmly attached to the tough, flexible soles."

(2) ONE WHIFF OF EXOTICA PERFUME
WILL PUT HIM UNDER YOUR SPELL

> What's $5 per ounce
> when your future's at stake?

Furthermore, the flacons are so exquisitely fashioned of cut glass that they make lovely conversation pieces for your dresser.

(3) XYZ'S M-80
WILL QUICKLY END
YOUR STICKY-VALVE WOES

> One 50¢ bottle of this potent
> additive will rid your engine of
> ping and increase its power.

Rough, noisy performance quickly succumbs to M-80. Just put a bottleful into your tank with every gas fill and forget those pesky valves.

(4) THE $45 SUIT WITH THE $75 LOOK
NOW ONLY $29.50 AT XYZ

> One-week introductory sale only!
> Every suit guaranteed finest
> tailoring, fit, style

Don't let a slim budget keep you from dressing well. XYZ suits are made from the same patterns as the most expensive custom models.

(5) NOW! SHEER NYLON
HOSIERY THAT WON'T
LADDER, RUN, OR STRETCH

Double your money back
if not as advertised

These marvelous products of a revolutionary knitting process
are exclusive in this city at XYZ.

HEADLINES SHOULD BE ACCURATE AND CONCRETE

Accuracy and concreteness should characterize all headlines.
Every ad should be judged according to these criteria, in addition
to those contained in the following evaluation chart:

Headlines (64%)

(1) Does the name of the advertiser appear within "eye range"
of the lead paragraph? (5%)

(2) Does the headline tell the prospect quickly and clearly the
main benefits to be obtained by buying, and does it identify the
product or service? (51%)

(3) Do the subheads in combination with the headline show the
reader exactly how or why he gets the promised benefits? (8%)

Body of Copy (36%)

(4) Do the first lines of copy develop the headlines? (20%)

(5) Does the succeeding copy support the headlines and first lines
of copy? (10%)

(6) Does the final paragraph ask for action or decision? (6%)

Chapter 10

ILLUSTRATIONS: THE FUNCTION OF THE PICTURE IS TO PROVIDE VISUAL PROOF OF COPY ASSERTIONS

ART SHOULD BE ORIGINAL OR SANCTIONED

Although it is debatable that a picture is worth a thousand words, the illustration is an essential ingredient of some advertisements and a contributing element of most.

In addition to reinforcing the copy, pictures of merchandise or services heighten the value of advertising in four distinct ways:

(1) Use of illustrations results in larger, more attractive (therefore more productive) ads and broadens the scope of space-selling opportunities.

(2) Pictures of merchandise or services on display or in use by students engaged in campus activities increase the pulling power, largely because of the interest generated by the personalities of the students pictured.

(3) The institutional value of advertising is enhanced by pictures of store fronts, display windows, store owners, managers, and clerks, and store name signs and slogans.

(4) Used sparingly, mortises, hand-lettered headlines, arrows, bullets, dots, clenched, upraised, or pointing hands, and other such attention-compelling and gaze-directing devices have telling effect on the appearance and readership of advertising.

Their function being to provide visual proof of assertions made in the copy, illustrations should be exact. For showing surface characteristics and action, therefore, the photograph is ideal. It is used extensively to illustrate clothing being modeled, cars and other ma-

99

chines being operated, and transactions occurring, and to identify signs, store fronts, personnel, and merchandise. (See Figs. 72-89.) As the illustrations demonstrate, line or halftone drawings may be more effective to reveal obscure or hidden detail, or to provide humor.

There is a tendency on the part of offset ad constructors to clip and use illustrations from publications other than their own. Unless permission of the publication in question has been obtained this is plagiarism, pure and simple, and the practitioner is literally begging for a suit at law.

Only original material should be used, which includes all that originated and provided by the advertiser.

It is a wise precaution to obtain permission of the subject of any photo used in an advertisement. (See Appendix G for standard photo release form.)

Illustrations should also be relevant to the subject. The temptation is strong among student advertising practitioners to depart from the central theme in the use of art. (See Fig. 89. Note how directly relevant the drawing is to the theme of Washington's Birthday.)

The photo and the drawing are ideal ad elements when the method of printing is offset, because engravings are not necessary. The drawing is laid into the paste-up and photographed with the rest of the copy. (See Fig. 90.) Only one additional step is required for the photo. A "window" is provided for it in the paste-up, which becomes a blank in the negative. (See Fig. 91.) The picture is then photographed through a screen so that its tonal qualities will be retained when transferred to the metal printing plate. It is then taped into place in the blank in the negative just before this transfer (called *burning*) takes place. (See Fig. 92.)

In letterpress printing, the use of original art and photos is more restricted. First, the cost of such illustrations and the necessary engravings is usually prohibitive, and second, often there is not time for this process. Most copy and layout work is produced close to deadline, usually from one to three days in advance.

Illustration Mat and Proof Services

The retail advertising profession almost universally subscribes to illustration and copy idea mat or reproduction proof services. (See Appendix H for list of companies providing these services.)

BOARED?

*the residence
halls
present
the 4th annual*

MARDI GRAS

**Saturday, March 14
7 p.m. - 1 a.m.
MARY WARD HALL**

**GAMES
REFRESHMENTS**
free — DANCE — live music

Fig. 72

Fig. 73

Fig. 82

Fig. 83

Fig. 84

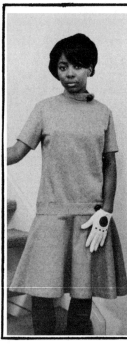

PARIS COMES TO BERKELEY

as a bonded jersey knit dress, modeled by L-11 Sherrion Ware.

The rayon and acrilic dress is available in both black/white and navy/red checks in sizes 7-16 for $29.

Her gloves in black or white are $3.

Fig. 85

L-11 Sue Carter Goes Mod !

in her dress by Susan Petites.

The skirt flares from dropped waist.

It has a rolled collar.

The colors are either orange and yellow or navy and red.

It is 100% acetate.

Price—$21.00
Sizes—3 to 15

Fig. 86

Fig. 87

CARTOONS
ENLIVEN
ADVERTISING

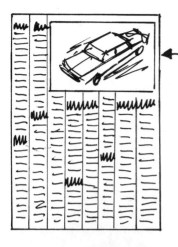

Fig. 90 Paste-up

Drawing pasted into page in same manner as the copy, and page photographed as a unit. The negative will then be ready for the burner.

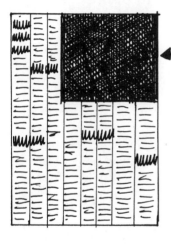

Fig. 91 Negative

"Window" of black paper pasted into page in same manner as copy and page photographed with this area blank. Photo illustration, having been made into a "screened" negative, will be taped into this space before page negative is ready to be burned.

Fig. 92 Negative

Screened negative of photo taped into window. Now the page is ready for burning (transfer to printing plate).

The illustration service is a large and complicated business. Literally thousands of artists, photographers, copy writers, layout specialists, engravers, printers, lithographers, researchers, and auditors work closely with merchandisers, retailers, manufacturers, wholesalers, and other distributors to provide illustrations and descriptions of thousands of items commonly found in retail display advertising in all consumer goods, service, and institutional categories, keyed to seasons of the year and geographical location.

In a typical "general" service, illustrations are provided in many sizes, some as large as a full newspaper page, others as small as ½″ x ½″. They are shown on the proof pages alone, in combination, and in suggested or model layouts, some complete with suggested copy.

These services may be obtained by subscription on almost any frequency basis, and a particular illustration may be ordered at any time—mats and proofs for letterpress and proofs only for offset printing. Some newspapers, especially small-town weeklies, subscribe on a four-times-a-year basis (Spring, Summer, Autumn, Winter), but most papers receive the service monthly. The proof books and/or corresponding mats arrive about the middle of the month before their suggested use.

Specialized services for groceries, drugs, furniture, jewelry, clothing, hardware, and many other retail classifications are available and are widely used by retailers who prepare their own ads. Other illustration services available to the retail advertising writer include manufacturers' and distributors' engravings, mats, or reproduction proofs and department store mats or repro proofs approved for re-use. (See Figs. 93, 94, 95a,b,c.)

How to Use the Illustration Service

The adman employs the illustration service in a multitude of ways.

First, for easy reference, he separates one or more of the proof books and inserts the pages according to subject in one or more post binder files.

Next, if his printing method is letterpress, he files the mats in numerical order corresponding with the numbers of the proofbook illustrations.

One or more of the proofbooks should be marked "No Clip," one or more marked "Clip," and one or more separated and filed.

Young fashions
"DRESS-UP"
for Easter
coats • suits • dresses

Young and gay every which-way . . .
for Easter, for Spring! The styles?
Choose from trim and tailored to
frisky and kooky. It's just a
marvelous year . . . to be you!

00⁰⁰ to 00⁰⁰

NAME

NAME

SWEATER SHIFT

"IN"
FOR
EASTER

her favorite

PANTSUIT

00⁰⁰

It's all the rage and as
"in" as can be! Boy
jackets, single or double,
and slim, slim slacks.

NAME

0⁰⁰

the wild and wonderful
SWEATER SHIFT

The "Swinger" look in a sweater shift, with the
pow of contrasting stripes. Styled in cotton in
poor boy or turtle-neck.

STAMPS • CONHAIM

Fig. 93

Fig. 94

Fig. 95a

Half-tone engraving mounted on type-high wood block.

TRUSTED FOR ACCURACY
SINCE 1853

TISSOT

STYLIST

$39⁹⁵

Classic, round stainless steel case.
Factory tested 17-jewel Tissot
movement . . . acclaimed for de-
pendability in 120 countries.

Lee-Frank
MANUFACTURING JEWELERS
MEMBER AMERICAN GEM SOCIETY
2210 SHATTUCK ● BERKELEY ● TH 3-6410

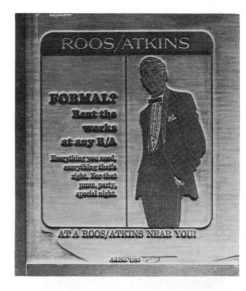

Fig. 95b   Mats of display advertisements

Fig. 95   Reproduction proof

Fig. 95c

The "dead metal" spaces between the illustrations on a mat page are half an inch in width. It is in these spaces that cutting should be done (as shown in Fig. 96). Each individual illustration is numbered, as is the page, for easy reference to the catalogued reproduction proof sheets, and for convenience of filing.

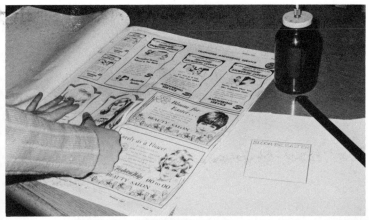

Fig. 96

Top—To make a layout for either "hot-type" composition or offset reproduction paste-up, requiring a service illustration, scissor desired picture from the proof page, cutting in the white separation spaces.

Center—Then trim the illustration and paste it into place in the layout. Use rubber cement. Some printers prefer that you indicate on the layout the area to be occupied by the picture and cement it on a separate piece of paper.

Below—To remove individual illustration from a mat page, cut in the middle of the "dead-metal" space.

Then he uses the service as a combination idea and illustration source. He looks through the file book for the illustration or copy idea he wants, then goes to the "Clip" book and cuts it out, taking care not to cut off the mat number. He next pastes the illustration into his layout, and either uses the accompanying copy (if any) as is, or adapts it. If his printing method is offset, the layout is ready for printing. Otherwise, he finds the corresponding mats of the illustration and cuts them out of the large mat page. (See Fig. 96.)

Care must be taken in this operation to cut in the center of the spaces (called "dead metal") between the illustrations so that the stereotypers will have room for the casting box bearers when the metal is cast. The constructor of the offset ad should leave space around the illustration when cutting it from the proof page, and postpone trimming until time of final paste-up.

It is most important for constructors of letterpress layouts to know that all adaptations of the illustration for layout purposes are accomplished in the printing department, not the advertising department. The mat is never to be altered. Even if only one square inch of a mat measuring a full page is to be used, if there are no dead-metal areas in which to cut, the entire mat is sent to the printer; he will cast it entire and then saw the desired part out of the metal, leaving the mat intact.

What happens is this:

The stereotyper casts the mat into a *stereo,* which is a type-high or shell (less than type-high) block of metal with the illustration transferred to its surface. Then he alters this cast in one of three ways to conform with the changes you may have made on the layout or proof:

(1) Cropping: sawing off unwanted parts.
(2) Routing: removing unwanted parts from the surface.
(3) Mortising: cutting a hole through the cast.

Incidentally, any art design such as a circle, triangle, or variation of the square or circle inside of which type or an illustration is placed is called a mortise.

Chapter 11

MEASUREMENT OF SPACE:
EVERYTHING MUST FIT

Sizing Standards Must Be Uniform, Exact

Reproducible, readable design being the objective of the advertising layout constructor, he must know the measurement system of his craft.

The elements must combine into an advertisement of a certain size and internal composition. The ad must fit into a page, which is also of a certain size and internal composition. The type and illustrations of a printed page are arranged in columns, varying from one or two in a yearbook or magazine, to as many as nine in a newspaper.

The present tendency of publications, in order to save paper, increase advertising rates, and improve the handling convenience of the product, is to reduce the width of the columns, the space between the columns, and the page.

The inch is the basic unit of vertical measurement of local advertising. Known as the *column inch,* it is a space 1 inch deep by 1 column wide. That is, an ad is so many column inches deep the long (vertical) way.

For horizontal (across columns) or page measurement, the column is used. Reference is to columns wide, or columns crossed.

For example, an advertisement 4 inches wide by 8 deep is not spoken of as 4 inches by 8 inches, but as 2 columns by 8 inches. The number of columns crossed always occurs first in the designation. (See Fig. 97.)

Multicolumn ads are always a little wider than the sum of columns crossed, because of the spaces separating the columns. But for purposes of clarity reference to this slight variable is omitted here. It will be referred to where it applies more specifically, later in the chapter.

The measurement unit of national advertising is the agate line, a term derived from agate type, which is 5½ points high. A column inch contains 14 agate lines; therefore, a 1-column by 2-inch ad is 28 agate lines, 1-column by 6-inches is 84 agate lines, and so on. To determine the size in lines of a multicolumn ad, multiply by the number of columns crossed, as with inches. A 3-column by 6-inch ad is 252 agate lines (6 x 14 x 3).

An insertion order from an agency for publication of a national advertisement will be specific as to the column width and depth in lines. The publisher's rate will take into account the width of the column, so that makes no difference. Column widths range from one and a half to three and a half inches in newspapers, and from two to eight inches in yearbooks and magazines.

The exact measurement of an ad is specified in various ways for the guidance of the person scheduling the lineage, dummying the paper, and marking the copy in the composing room. As discussed earlier, one way is to write it on the layout sheet, and another is to fill out an insertion order to be attached to the layout sheet.

VISUALIZED FORMS ARE MORE MEANINGFUL

The best way to understand the relationship of ads to editorial content is to consider them as spaces or units on a page. Thus visualized in context, their forms become more meaningful, the details of their construction more pertinent, and it can be seen why certain arrangements of elements are more effective than others or more appropriate for the purpose intended.

It is also easier to understand in this manner how many ads can be placed on a page and how they appear in various positions, sizes, and shapes.

Therefore it behooves the advertising practitioner to make a close study of sizes, shapes, and positions in order to make the most effective use of the resources at his disposal.

Other than the column inch and agate line, space units are segments of the page: 1/32, 1/16, 1/8, 1/4, 1/2, and 3/4 page, full page, double truck (center spread of two facing pages) and four-page section in one unit of two pages of paper. As the space widths

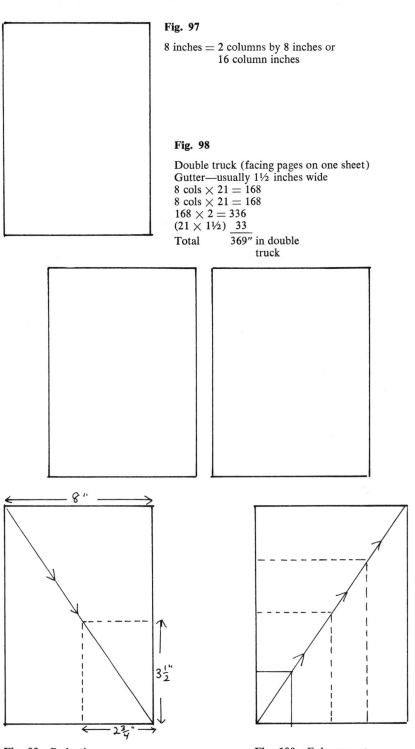

Fig. 97

8 inches = 2 columns by 8 inches or
16 column inches

Fig. 98

Double truck (facing pages on one sheet)
Gutter—usually 1½ inches wide
8 cols × 21 = 168
8 cols × 21 = 168
168 × 2 = 336
(21 × 1½) 33
Total   369″ in double
                     truck

Fig. 99   Reduction

Fig. 100   Enlargement

increase, more attention must be paid to the corresponding size of the layout, because as columns are crossed the amount of column rule space becomes more significant, and the gutter on the double truck makes a considerable difference. (See Fig. 98.)

In addition to greater economy of space utilization through more precise arrangement of layout elements and of the ad itself within the dummy, another reason for exact measurement is to help the printer be more accurate in composition and make-up. Nothing is more costly in terms of time, money, and temper than trying to compose an ad with the wrong sizes of type and illustrations, which happens when the incorrectly sized layout is taken literally. The printer should be able to take the layout literally. It is a time-honored rule for him always to "follow copy."

SOME PRINTING TERMS AND TECHNIQUES

Although the advertising practitioner may not need the information often, he should know some of the techniques and terms employed by the printer. The typesetter or compositor may refer to the line gauge or "pica pole," for example. This is a metal ruler calibrated in picas and points. A pica is established at 1/6 inch; it is used for measuring width. A point is 1/72 inch and is used to measure depth, thickness of rules, borders, and height of type: 72 points is one inch, 36 is half inch, 18 is quarter inch, and so on. Text type ranges from 5 to 12 point, and display from 12 to 108, sometimes larger. "Type high," the distance from the bottom of the base to the printing surface of type, is .918 inch.

Suppose the printer says: "There is room in that ad for a copy block 12 picas wide by 288 points deep." A quick bit of figuring tells you that the "hole" is 2 inches wide by 4 inches deep (12 divided by 6 and 288 divided by 72).

Or he says: "Make that cut 24 picas wide by 216 points deep." You mark the photo or drawing for an engraving or have it drawn or trim it for a paste-up 4 inches wide by 3 inches deep.

HOW TO SCALE FOR REDUCTION AND ENLARGEMENT

In order to plan the layout, it is necessary to know what size the illustrations will be when reduced or enlarged. The four methods of enlarging and reducing (scaling) photographs or other illustrations (copy and layout, too, in the offset process) are mathematical calculation, photocopy, diagonal line, and camera lucida, in which an image is projected by a lens and then traced. The diagonal line method is used most frequently because it is fast and accurate enough for all practical purposes. An 8 x 10-inch illustration is to be reduced to 6 inches wide. How deep will it be?

Do this: Lay out an 8-inch by 10-inch space (or the area desired plus margins) and run a diagonal line with a ruler from upper left to lower right corner. Now measure the width desired (in this case 6 inches) on the bottom boundary from the right margin and draw a line from that point up to the diagonal. The depth of the engraving will be the distance from the bottom boundary to the intersection. (See Fig. 99.)

To enlarge: Lay out a lateral the width of the illustration, copy block, or layout, and an indefinite vertical line at right angles to it. Lay the area in the angle and run a diagonal from lower left corner to upper right corner and on out to meet the opposite vertical. The distance from this point of intersection to the boundary will be the height of the printed illustration. (See Fig. 100.)

Often, in offset, the printer will prefer 1/3 or 1/5 scaling. In this case calculate mathematically by making the design to be scaled proportionately smaller or larger than it will be when printed.

Chapter 12

COPY FITTING: IT TAKES A BIT OF FIGURING

THE PROCESS IS ONE OF EQUATION

Copy fitting is the process of equating typewritten or handwritten copy with type. Because type varies so much in size, this equation is essential. Only so many characters of any given size will fit into a given space. Type cannot be stretched or squeezed. Only minimum adjustment is possible by spacing techniques.

Most practitioners hand-letter major headlines in their layouts and indicate the copy lines and blocks by straight or wavy lines. Then they measure the space for copy and write it to fit on a typewriter. (See Fig. 101.)

LINE-FOR-LINE METHOD IS PROBABLY THE EASIEST

The following line-for-line method is probably the easiest way to produce typed copy that will fit a certain space when it is set in type:

(1) Measure the width of the type line. Select the size and style of type desired and count the number of its characters in a line of this width. Count each space and punctuation mark as a character.

(2) Adjust typewriter to type exactly this number of characters on a line. The total number of both typing and type will then be the same. In other words, the copy is typed line for line; a line of typed copy will make a line of printer's type.

(3) To find the number of lines of type required to fill a certain space, first determine the *body* size. This may be different from the *face* size. For example: A 10-point type face may be set on a 12-point body, in order to put more space between the lines. There being 72 points to the inch, determine the number of lines to the inch by

dividing 72 by the body size. Thus, if the body size is 12 point, divide 72 by 12, for a result of 6 lines to the inch. Then to find the total number of lines needed, multiply the number of lines per inch by the depth of the type area, measured in inches. Make allowance for headings and illustrations. The following scale will assist you:

Point size of type body	6	7	8	9	10	11	12	14	18
Number of lines per inch	12	10	9	8	7	6½	6	5	4

(4) Type the copy a little short of the space indicated to allow for a slight variation in character count.

(5) If the copy is typed line for line and you wish to find out how much space it will take when set in type, divide the total number of typed lines by the number of lines of type per inch in the size you have selected. For example: There may be 84 lines of copy typed line for line to be set in 8-point type on a 10-point body. There are approximately 7 lines of a 10-point body type per inch (see scale above); dividing 84 by 7, you find that the copy will fill a space 12″ deep.

(6) To convert inches to picas, merely multiply the number of inches by 6, as there are 6 picas to the inch.

(7) To determine the number of words in a manuscript, count the words in three typical lines and divide that total by 3 to get the average per line. Then multiply this average by the total number of lines in the manuscript.

(8) To find the number of pages of type required for a manu-

Fig. 101

There being six lines of 12-pt. type to each inch of depth, you will type 18 lines to fill the three inches of space. The factor for 12 pt. is 1.75 characters to the pica. There are six picas to the inch so each line will contain 21 characters. Set typewriter bar from 10 to 31 and type 18 lines. This will result in 18 lines of 12-pt. type.

It is your life and the lives of your loved ones that are at stake. Don't endanger them by driving on worn, unsafe tires. Come in today and let us equip your car with puncture-resistant Safety-Treads.

A moment's inspection of a cut-away section of a safety tread will convince you. So unique is the woven steel and fabric construction, it is protected by patent. No other tire is remotely like it.

Many owners report their Safety-Treads have lasted 50,000 miles without going flat. You, too, can enjoy the sense of security such performance assures.

Here is life insurance at no extra premium as Safety-Treads are competitively priced. Come in and let us demonstrate.

30-, 60-, 90-day charge accounts invited. Time payments arranged to suit your budget. Open daily 6 to 10.

Fig. 102

1050 typewritten characters set in 8-pt. type on 9-pt. slug (factor: 8 pt. = 3.25) will result in a copy block 3½ inches (20 picas) wide by 2 inches deep.

17 lines × 9 pts. = 153 pts. ÷ 72 (pts. to inch) = 2″

script typed line for line, determine the number of lines of type on a page and divide the total number of lines in the manuscript by this figure.

(9) The following is a good rule-of-thumb chart to determine the number of words to the square inch of an average type:

5-pt. solid	5-pt. leaded	6-pt. solid	6-pt. leaded	8-pt. solid	8-pt. leaded
69	50	47	34	32	23

10-pt. solid	10-pt. leaded	12-pt. solid	12-pt. leaded
21	16	14	11

ANOTHER WAY IS BY CHARACTER COUNT

Suppose the copy manuscript is 21 lines, 5 inches wide, in pica typewriter type, which contains 10 characters to the inch. To find the number of characters, multiply 5″ by 10 by 21:

10 characters to the inch in pica (elite is 12 to the inch)
x5 inches
───
50 characters to the line
x21 lines
───
1,050 characters

Because the letters of type do not all occupy uniform spaces across a page, and because they may be smaller or larger than typewritten characters, type manufacturers compute the average number of characters that a given type will occupy in a pica of measure. This is called the factor of type. (Caution: This pica is a measurement; that of the typewriter is a style.)

This means that a type face with a factor of 3.25 will average 3.25 characters for each pica of space across a page. For example, a 20-pica measure will accommodate 65 characters.

Now, the 1,050 characters (in the previously mentioned 5 inch by 21 line manuscript page) divided by the 65 characters of printing type in a 20-pica measure (as derived from the factor) will give the number of lines of type contained in the page of typewritten script: 1,050 divided by 65 equals 16.16, or 17 lines of type.

To find the depth in inches, bear in mind that there are 72 points to the inch, 12 points to the pica or em (1/6″), and 6 picas to the inch, and that points are used in vertical, picas in hoizontal, measurement.

Depth in inches of the foregoing example, assuming the type is set on 9-point body (slug) is determined by multiplying the number of lines by the depth of the slug: 9 times 17 equals 153 points.

The point total divided by the points to the line equals 2 inches plus one line: 153 divided by 72 equals 2 inches 9 points (or 1 line).

Therefore, the 1,050 manuscript characters of pica typewriter type set in printers' 8-point type on a 9-point slug, at 20 picas of measure (3⅓ inches) with a factor of 3.25 per pica will be 2 inches deep. (See Fig. 102.)

Note: In this case the printers' type was 8-point, because this has a 3.25 factor and will fit on a 9-point slug.

OR TRY IT THIS WAY, USING THE SAMPLE SHEET

A simple way used by many advertising writers is the following:

Have the printer set up a sample sheet of all the type faces and sizes in the shop (see Fig. 103), or of those you will be using. Then

This Type Is 8 Point Vogue Extra Bold — Now is the time for all good men to come to the aid of
This Type Is 8 Point Vogue Medium — Now is the time for all good men to come to the aid of
ABCDEFGHIJKLMNOPQRSTUVWXYZ—NOW IS THE TIME FOR ALL GOOD MEN TO COME T
abcdefghijklmnopqrstuvwxyz—now is the time for all good men to come to the aid of their coun

This Type Is 6 Point Vogue Extra Bold — Now is the time for all good men to come to the aid of their country.
This Type Is 6 Point Vogue Medium — Now is the time for all good men to come to the aid of their country.
ABCDEFGHIJKLMNOPQRSTUVWXYZ—NOW IS THE TIME FOR ALL GOOD MEN TO COME TO THE AID OF
abcdefghijklmnopqrstuvwxyz—now is the time for all good men to come to the aid of their country now is th

This Type Is 12 Point Scotch — Now is the time for all good men to
This Type Is 12 Point Scotch Italic — Now is the time for all good me
THIS TYPE IS 12 POINT SCOTH WITH CAPS AND SMALL CAPS — Now
ABCDEFGHIJKLMNOPQRSTUVWXYZ—NOW IS THE
abcdefghijklmnopqrstuvwxyz—now is the time for all good men to co

This Type Is 12 Point Baskerville — Now is the time for all good men
This Type Is 12 Point Baskerville Italic — Now is the time for all good
THIS TYPE IS 12 POINT BASKERVILLE CAPS AND SMALL CAPS—NOW IS TH
ABCDEFGHIJKLMNOPQRSTUVWXYZ—NOW IS THE TIME F
abcdefghijklmnopqrstuvwxyz—now is the time for all good men to com

This Type Is 10 Point Baskerville — Now is the time for all good men to come to
This Type Is 10 Point Baskerville Italic — Now is the time for all good men to
THIS TYPE IS 10 POINT BASKERVILLE CAPS AND SMALL CAPS — NOW IS THE TIME FOR
ABCDEFGHIJKLMNOPQRSTUVWXYZ—NOW IS THE TIME FOR ALL G
abcdefghijklmnopqrstuvwxyz—now is the time for all good men to come to the ai

This Type Is 8 Point Baskerville — Now is the time for all good men to come to the aid of their
This Type is 8 Point Baskerville Italic — Now is the time for all good men to come to the aid of
THIS TYPE IS 8 POINT BASKERVILLE CAPS AND SMALL CAPS — NOW IS THE TIME FOR ALL GOOD MEN TO
ABCDEFGHIJKLMNOPQRSTUVWXYZ—NOW IS THE TIME FOR ALL GOOD MEN TO C
abcdefghijklmnopqrstuvwxyz—now is the time for all good men to come to the aid of their coun

This Type Is 10 Point Century Bold — Now is the time for all good men to
This Type Is 10 Point Century Light — Now is the time for all good men to
ABCDEFGHIJKLMNOPQRSTUVWXYZ—NOW IS THE TIME FOR ALL
abcdefghijklmnopqrstuvwxyz—now is the time for all good men to come to

This Type Is 12 Point Memphis Bold — Now is the time for all good
This Type Is 12 Point Memphis Light — Now is the time for all
ABCDEFGHIJKLMNOPQRSTUVWXYZ—NOW IS THE TIME FOR
abcdefghijklmnopqrstuvwxyz—now is the time for all good men t

This Type Is 10 Point Memphis Bold — Now is the time for all good men to come
This Type Is 10 Point Memphis Light — Now is the time for all good men to come
ABCDEFGHIJKLMNOPQRSTUVWXYZ—NOW IS THE TIME FOR ALL GOOD
abcdefghijklmnopqrstuvwxyz—now is the time for all good men to come to the

This Type Is 9 Point Excelsior Bold — Now is the time for all good men to come
This Type Is 9 Point Excelsior Light — Now is the time for all good men to come
ABCDEFGHIJKLMNOPQRSTUVWXYZ—NOW IS THE TIME FOR ALL GOO
abcdefghijklmnopqrstuvwxyz—now is the time for all good men to come to the

This Type is 7 Point (8) Excelsior Bold—Now is the time for all good men to come to th
This Type is 7 Point (8) Excelsior Light — Now is the time for all good men to come to th
ABCDEFGHIJKLMNOPQRSTUVWXYZ—NOW IS THE TIME FOR ALL GOOD MEN TO
abcdefghijklmnopqrstuvwxyz—now is the time for all good men to come to the aid of thei

Fig. 103

count the number of characters and spaces in any desired width. Set the typewriter space bar to this figure, and write as many lines as the depth of space will permit.

For example: You have a typed page of ad copy containing 20 seven-inch lines. You want it set 15 picas (2½ inches) wide in 12-point type. The result will be 34 lines of type (6.8 inches); the typewriter stop setting will be 26.25. Try it and see.

Formula: 1.75 characters to the pica (12-point type) times 15 picas or 2½ inches to the line equals 26.25 characters to the line.

To find the number of lines, measure the depth of the page, then multiply by points to the inch and divide by 14 (depth of line plus 2 points of lead or spacing):

$$
\begin{array}{l}
72 \quad \text{points} \\
\underline{\text{x}6\tfrac{1}{2} \quad \text{inches (20 double-spaced lines)}} \\
468 \quad \text{points}
\end{array}
$$

468 divided by 14 equals 33.4 lines in 12-point type; and 33.4 divided by 5 lines to the inch equals 6.8 inches depth.

Chapter 13

*TYPOGRAPHY: ITS PURPOSE IS TO MAKE
ADVERTISING EASIER TO READ*

Style of Type Should Be Appropriate

The purpose of typography (the art of type and its arrangement) is to make advertising easier to read. Therefore, the advertising practitioner should be thoroughly familiar with the various type faces.

The style of type chosen should be appropriate to the advertising. At the most elementary level this would mean large, bold type for an automobile ad and a small, graceful face for a dainty gown or bottle of perfume. However, this is oversimplification. Experience with type will reveal a myriad adaptations of the typographical idea.

As a rule choice of the exact type for the ad is best left to the printer. This is especially true when the print shop is small and has few and incomplete faces and sizes of type, or when the advertising writer is inexperienced in typography and copy fitting or does not know what types are available to the printer.

However, the expert advertising practitioner will be adept at both arts. They are really quite simple and should be learned well in the beginning.

The best sources for type faces—historic and current—are the type catalogs published by Mergenthaler Linotype Company, Intertype Corporation, McKenzie & Harris, American Type Founders, or other type manufacturers, and textbooks on typography.

In order to work competently with type, knowledge of sizes is more important than that of faces. You should hear the wailing and gnashing of teeth in the printing shops of the world as ill-fitting copy pours in!

Type height is measured in points and ranges from 5 to 108. Five-point type is about 1/15 inch and is called minion; 5½-point is called agate and at 14 to the inch is the universal unit of advertising measurement; 108-point type is 1½ inches high and is variously called "Boxcar," "Railroad," or "Studhorse." In-between sizes are 6, 8, 9, 10, 11, 12, 14, 18, 24, 30, 36, 42, 48, 60, 72, 84, and 96. Most body type, or that used for columnar and copy block material, is 6, 8, 9, 10, and 11 points in height. Minion and agate are seldom used. The larger sizes, called "display," are employed for headlines and display lines. (See Fig. 104.)

Advertising utilizes all sizes and faces of type in all styles: "down," or lower case (LC); "up," capitals or upper case (UC); or both up and down, capitals and lower case (U&LC). For example:

THIS LINE IS IN UPPER CASE
this line is in lower case
This Line Is in Upper and Lower Case

Instructions written on the advertising layout and copy sheets for the guidance of printers are called "mark-up." These notations include face, size, style, and placement of type. (See Fig. 105.)

If the advertising writer knows how and the print shop has enough variety of type to fulfill the requirements, he does the mark-up. Otherwise a properly executed layout will tell the printer the over-all effect desired, and he will use the faces and sizes most likely to achieve it.

The basic unit of type measurement being the point (1/72 inch), it follows that 8-point type will set 9 lines to the inch; 10-point, 7.2 lines; 14-point, 5.14 lines, and so forth, set solid. When type is set solid, the type occupies the full thickness of the body (base or slug). Adjustment between hot-type (cast in metal) lines is achieved with 1-point leads and with spacing regulator on the justifying typewriter or other cold-type machines. (See Appendix J.)

For example: There are six lines of 10-point type with 2-point interlinear spacing in one inch (72 divided by 10 plus 2 equals 6).

The most readable line lengths are: 9 to 13 picas (1½ to 2⅙ inches) in 8-point; 13 to 19 picas (2⅙ to 3⅙ inches) in 10-point; and so on up the scale in jumps of four picas. The pica, at 6 to the inch, should be remembered as the basic horizontal type measurement unit.

This Type Is 4 Point Century Exp with Gothic — Now is the time for all good men to come
This Type Is 4 Point Century Exp with Gothic — Now is the time for all good men to come
ABCDEFGHIJKLMNOPQRSTUVWXYZ—NOW IS THE TIME FOR ALL GOOD MEN TO COME
abcdefghijklmnopqrstuvwxyz—now is the time for all good men to come to the aid of the

6 Pt. Franklin Gothic Extra Condensed

How is one to assess and evaluate a type face in terms of its esthetic design? Why do

HOW IS ONE TO ASSESS AND EVALUATE A TYPE FACE IN TERMS OF ITS ESTHETIC

8 Pt. Franklin Gothic Extra Condensed

How is one to assess and evaluate a type face in terms of its esthetic d

HOW IS ONE TO ASSESS AND EVALUATE A TYPE FACE IN TERMS OF IT

10 Pt. Franklin Gothic Extra Condensed

How is one to assess and evaluate a type face in terms of it

HOW IS ONE TO ASSESS AND EVALUATE A TYPE FACE IN

12 Pt. Franklin Gothic Extra Condensed

How is one to assess and evaluate a type face in terms

HOW IS ONE TO ASSESS AND EVALUATE A TYPE FA

14 Pt. Franklin Gothic Extra Condensed

How is one to assess and evaluate a type face

HOW IS ONE TO ASSESS AND EVALUATE A T

18 Pt. Franklin Gothic Extra Condensed

How is one to assess and evaluate a ty

HOW IS ONE TO ASSESS AND EVALU

24 Pt. Franklin Gothic Extra Condensed

How is one to assess and eval

HOW IS ONE TO ASSESS AND

30 Pt. 20th Century Extrabold Condensed

How is one to assess an

HOW IS ONE TO AS

36 Pt. Spartan Black

How is one to

HOW IS ONE

How is one to
HOW IS ONE T

How is or
HOW IS

How is one
HOW IS O

Fig. 104

1/18 of an inch high
1/9 of an inch
1/4 of an inch
1/2 of an inch

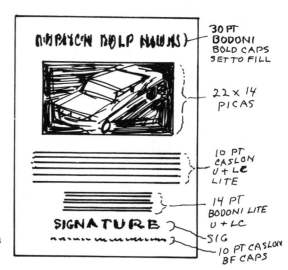

30 PT BODONI BOLD CAPS SET TO FILL

22 x 14 PICAS

10 PT CASLON U + LC LITE

14 PT BODONI LITE U + LC

SIG

10 PT CASLON BF CAPS

Fig. 105

2/3 of an inch
One inch

Twelve-point type is considered to be the most readable size if proportionately leaded (line spaced).

How Style Is Achieved

Styling in advertising typography derives from internally consistent and externally appropriate composition, all of which is achieved by discriminating choice of type faces and sizes and arrangement of layout elements.

For example:

(1) Headlines may be

(a) set full length

HEADLINES MAY BE
SET   FULL   LENGTH

(b) Set flush left

HEADLINES MAY BE
SET FLUSH LEFT

(c) Set flush right

HEADLINES MAY BE
SET   FLUSH   RIGHT

(d) Centered

HEADLINES MAY BE
CENTERED

(e) Up

HEADLINES MAY BE
UP—ALL CAPITALS

(f) down

headlines may be
down—lower case

(g) UP and down

Headlines May Be
Up and Down

(h) One, two, three, or more lines, one or more columns

HEADLINES MAY BE SET FULL PAGE WIDTH

Headlines May Be Set in
Any Number of Columns

headlines may be
set one column
one line, two lines,
three or more lines

(2) Subheads may be set in the same manner and also "run in" (first line indented, the rest flush left). For example:

HEADLINES MAY BE
SET FULL LENGTH

Some typographers think this is a more attractive style than flush or center.

(3) The copy block may be:

(a) First line flush left with the rest indented (hanging indentation).
For example:

These shirts are carefully tailored
of fine broadcloth, preshrunk,
and yours for a less-than-cost
price because they are slightly
soiled.

(b) First paragraph flush left, following ones indented:

These shirts are carefully tailored
of fine broadcloth, preshrunk, and

yours for a less-than-cost price because they are slightly soiled.

Come in today for yours. At
five for $10, why not stock up for
the future?

(c)   All lines flush left:

These shirts are carefully tailored
of fine broadcloth, preshrunk, and
yours for a less-than-cost price
because they are slightly soiled.

Come in today for yours. At five
for $10, why not stock up for the
future?

(d)   All lines flush right:

These shirts are carefully
tailored of fine broadcloth,
preshrunk, and yours for a
less-than-cost price because
they are slightly soiled.

(e)   Each paragraph indented:

These shirts are carefully
tailored of fine broadcloth, preshrunk, and yours for a less-than-
cost price because they are slightly
soiled.

Come in today for yours. At
five for $10, why not stock up for
the future?

(f)   Formally or irregularly staggered lines:

These shirts are carefully
tailored of fine broadcloth,
preshrunk, and yours for a

less-than-cost price because
they are slightly soiled.

or

These shirts are carefully
tailored of fine broadcloth,
preshrunk, and yours for a
less-than-cost price because
they are slightly soiled.

(g) All sentences flush right and left (squared):

These shirts are carefully
tailored of fine broadcloth,
preshrunk, and yours for a
less-than-cost price because
they are slightly soiled.

(4) The service copy (such as phone number, address, room or floor number, store hours, coupon, etc.) should not detract from the selling message or overshadow the signature. It should be placed inconspicuously.

(5) Price should be emphasized only to the degree that it is a selling point.

(6) It is best to integrate the signature into the layout in such a way as to neither dominate nor be submerged. This may be done by incorporation into headline or artwork.

The signature placed at the top of the layout tends to stop readership at that point. As in news, who is talking is not as important to the reader as what is said. In news writing, however, the "what" may stand alone without a source other than the observer, but this is never true in advertising. The "who" must always be plainly stated; in addition to the fact that "who" pays for the "what," the advertisement would be nonsensical without a source. (See Figs. 106-111.)

OFFSET ALLOWS FOR STYLE FLEXIBILITY

The process of constructing advertising for offset reproduction differs little from that for letterpress. The copy-writing differs not at all, but disposition of the elements in layout is more flexible.

Fig. 106   BAD—Firm name overwhelms the ad.

Fig. 107   BETTER—Firm name within eye range of headline.

Fig. 108   BEST—Firm name incorporated into headline.

Fig. 109   BAD—Price too prominent. Should be de-emphasized in quality copy.

Fig. 110   BAD—Service copy such as store hours, credit policy, should be inconspicuous in merchandising layout.

Fig. 111   BETTER—Below, above or alongside firm name except when service is theme of ad.

Fig. 112   Type over illustration.

Fig. 113   Curved lines. Type over illustration.

Fig. 114   Angled illustrations and copy blocks or boxes.

OFFSET	LETTERPRESS

OFFSET

1. Same

2. Type is set as in letterpress and proofs are pulled, or on justifying typewriter, filmstrip or sensitized paper.

3. Elements (proofs of type, illustrations or original typewritten material, and "windows" for photos) are pasted into place according to layout and directly into page according to dummy.

LETTERPRESS

1. Advertisement is prepared with pencil and typewriter—copy on one sheet and layout on another.

2. Type is set by hand or on type-casting machine.

3. Ad is composed by hand according to layout with metal elements—type, spacing and border material, zinc or copper engravings.

Fig. 115 Printer composes ad

Fig. 116 Ad is "pasted up" on light table

4. Ad is put into place in page according to dummy. When all type is composed into page, it is "justified" (adjusted to fit), and locked up (tightened).

4. Ad elements are pasted into place according to layout on a sheet of paper corresponding in size and style to the final printed version which is taped onto a sheet of glass lighted from beneath.

LETTERPRESS

Fig. 117 Page is made up on stone

5. It is then either placed on a flatbed printing press or a "mat" (cardboard impression) is made of it. This mat is then cast into a metal cylinder for rotary method printing. In either case, printing is directly from face of type to paper.

OFFSET

Fig. 118 Photographer "shoots" paste-up

5. The film negative that results from this operation is developed in the darkroom. It is then taped into a frame of stiff paper and screened negatives of photos taped into the windows. Finally it is "touched up" (imperfections corrected).

OFFSET

Fig. 119 Negative is burned into plate

6. Negative is placed on a thin sheet of metal and put into "burner," (cabinet equipped with electric heating element). Heat is applied for one minute. This "melts" negative onto the plate.

Fig. 120 Plate is washed

6. The plate is sponged with chemical solution which causes image to appear on surface. It is then placed on cylinder press for printing.

Fig. 121

Fig. 122

Fig. 123

The layout for offset permits almost any imaginable arrangement of the elements.

For example, type may be superimposed over the illustrations and copy and illustrations may be incorporated in many ways. (See Figs. 112, 113, 114.)

Even when copy is set by linecasting machines, except in the process of pulling proofs, no metal is involved in the composition of offset advertising. When the type is set by justifying typewriters or photographic devices, and original illustrations and proofs supplied by advertisers are used, no metal at all is handled.

Following is a step-by-step illustrated comparison of the letterpress and offset methods. (See Figs. 115-123.) In Appendix K is a list of rules for better typography.

Chapter 14

COLOR BENEFITS ADVERTISER
AND PUBLICATION ALIKE

COLOR OUTPULLS BLACK AND WHITE

Inasmuch as color in advertising outpulls black and white about 66 to 1, according to most studies, it should be offered to clients by those publications printed in shops that can produce it. The benefits are better results for the advertiser and greater profits for the publication. (See Fig. 124.)

Although color increases the pulling power of copy and layout, the ad must be good to start with. Color alone will not redeem it.

The use of color varies with the product. It is best employed for realism; *i.e.,* to illustrate colored products.

First, the color should be appropriate; that is: (1) scientifically correct, (2) realistic, and (3) aesthetically pleasing.

Next, regional color preferences should be observed. For example, research has proved that there are certain national favorites—such as ivory, pale green, blue, pink, and yellow—as well as geographical variances known only from local experience.

Generally speaking, these variables depend on weather. The amount of sunshine is the key: The brighter the region, the brighter the colors preferred, and vice versa.

From the foregoing, the reason for color must be obvious. To be read, an ad first must be noticed, and thus the first job of color is to attract attention. This it does by brightness or contrast.

Another factor is pleasure, induced in the reader by aesthetic colors and blends.

The third of this trio of reasons, realism, should perhaps be first. Experience has proved that it is the colored portrayal of colored merchandise that enhances the pulling power of color advertising. Generally, red and yellow are the best attention-getters. The reigning favorites are red (exciting), green (tranquil), blue (subduing), and yellow (cheerful).

The primary colors are red, yellow, and blue; the secondary colors are orange, green, and violet.

For most of us, color is a major psychological factor in daily living, shaping our moods and ideas from morning until night. We are affected by the colors we choose for our homes, our cars, our offices, even our toothpastes and foods. Nearly every product we buy has color, and more often than not color affects our buying decisions. Advertisers have long realized the psychological advantages of using color in presenting their products. At great expense they add color to their advertising as well as their products.

However, few professional advertising people, let alone teachers and advisers, have progressed in knowledge of color application beyond the attention-compelling stage. It takes training to produce effective color advertising. At what point should such instruction start?

First, the advertising copy writer and layout maker must understand the relationship of color to the product being advertised.

Second, he must know something about color itself.

Third, he must know the characteristics of the particular segment of the buying public he is trying to reach.

Every advertising practitioner should be equipped with a book or chart (available from ink manufacturers) showing the basic colors and formulas for the many color variations. The basic colors in any book or chart are the primaries—red, yellow, blue—from which all variations are derived with the help of white. He must then learn the nature of these colors in order to apply them properly.

Color Should Relate to the Product

Color should be the same as that of the product. Usually, however, the adman must lay out an ad with mats or cuts not having color plate additions, making it almost impossible to put color into the illustration itself. Here a wise use of color elsewhere in the layout can often convey the idea of the color of the product. When this is not of

Fig. 124

Fig. 125

Fig. 126

Fig. 127

Fig. 128

Fig. 129

DONT

OK

OVRACNDP

Fig. 130

primary concern, then type colors must be carefully chosen to enhance the very nature of the product itself. (See Figs. 125, 126.)

For instance, the layout displays gay summer wear for girls and the mat illustrations do not have color plates. Use a colored headline or border, or a tintblock under the type. Because women's summer wear usually carries an abundance of warm, exciting colors, you should not use cold colors. Bright red, orange, or yellow would be better related to the product. If, on the other hand, you are laying out an ad for garden produce, green would be an ideal choice. It identifies with the product.

A sale ad, in which many products are displayed, requires exciting colors to make the items seem genuine bargains. One does not identify blue or green with the stimulation a sale should have. Rather, hot reds or bright yellows get the point across much better. In ads for lingerie or cosmetics the identification would be with something soft and feminine. Choose the colors closest to the milder pastel shades. Although it is not always possible, try to pick colors that will not clash with the nature of the product.

COLORS HAVE IMPACT

Where color is to be used for attention-getting purposes without product identification, one must consider which colors will effectively do the job. The screaming vibrance of red, used in abundance, will certainly draw attention to a sale ad. The reader is jolted to reaction by the dramatic impact. But certainly, a bank should not use great quantities of red; it would not convey the dignity associated with finance. A small, subtle use of red, however, might emphasize the bank's message, though even in this use red is not usually a good prestige color. (See Figs. 127, 128.)

Every color has a different impact on the reader. Blue and red will make headings or prices stand out or lend great emphasis to any part of an ad. When the ad layout does not have an area open to large uses of color, bright yellow can be effective. As all sizes of type can be read easily when printed over yellow, large areas of this surprisingly bright color will lend great impact. Yellow can also be used effectively in quantity in prestige advertising. If the effect is to be more subtle, other colors of varying degrees of brightness should be used, particularly where dignity and quality are concerned. The impact of lighter colors should be secondary to the message.

COLORS CAN INDUCE MOOD

Color advertising has a distinct advantage over black and white not only because of eye appeal but also because it can put the reader into the mood for a certain product.

For example, pastels in cosmetics and intimate apparel appeal to the feminine ego, the idea being that soft colors imply soft things. Strong colors are exciting and should be used with an equally exciting product or idea.

The wrong colors produce adverse effects, especially in food advertising. Green, for example, is psychologically wrong in meat advertising but ideal for some vegetables. When using color in a food ad, keep in mind the colors of the *food on your plate*. Reds, yellows, and greens predominate, and you should use these colors whenever possible. As no set rules govern the ideal color for every product, you must learn through observation and use the colors or combination of colors most suitable in each case.

The principles of color layout are much the same as for black and white. Neatness and ample copy space are of prime importance. If the basic layout is poor, color will only add to the reader's difficulties. The same bad effect can be achieved by indiscriminate use of color in a basically good layout. So it is important to consider how you are going to use color before the layout is started.

Do you want to emphasize certain elements or ideas in the ad, or do you want to use color as an attention compeller only? Is the advertiser trying to publicize a big sale event, or to point out the quality or desirability of his product? These things must be considered in the same terms as when writing the black-and-white ad, the difference being the integration of color in harmonious balance with the layout. How a layout in black and white and in color are basically the same is shown in Fig. 124.

As an aid in formulating your color layouts, the illustration services provide excellent mats that can be used in black only or in black and color in many variations.

HOW TO LAY OUT A COLOR AD

Following is a step-by-step method of laying out a color ad:

(1) Visualize the finished advertisement and choose the colors to be used. *Think!*

(2) Gather together all your color tools, background mats, and other ingredients you will use.

(3) Sketch your ad out lightly with pencil to determine the basic layout. With colored pencils, pastels or marking pen, block in the color, following the pencil markings. Remember, dark colors such as red, blue, and green should not be used under type or illustrations, as they tend to make black hard to see. A dark color should be used for headings, border, price, or anywhere by itself where it can be emphasized and will not detract from copy. Caution should also be observed when using dark color in halftone, it being too strong for most copy overprinting. (See Figs. 129, 130.)

Copy should be printed over a dark color only when type is big and bold as in a headline. In good layouts the color, if strong, should be kept well away from body copy. If color is too close, the eye is distracted from the message. However, large masses of color such as yellow or any of the light pastels can be used under the black copy with good results. Here again, the small body copy is more effective if kept away from the color. Where background illustrations of different shapes are to be used under black type, it is better to trace the outline and fill it in with color than to paste down the mat illustration proof and then attempt to color it. This results in a much neater layout and makes it easier for the typesetter to understand what you want. If your layout requires a great deal of mat service paste-up as in a black-and-white ad, it is far simpler to make a complete black-and-white sketch and then indicate color areas on a tissue overlay.

(4) Don't overuse color. Too much can be disastrous. Remember, it is not color you are selling, but the product. Color is only a way of helping to sell it. Generally, simplified use of color is most effective. When indicating type matter for color, keep in mind that small faces are difficult to read in color. Most pastels should not be used for type matter even in the large faces.

(5) After color has been blocked in, prepare the complete black-and-white phase of the layout. Examine the results to see if all copy can be easily read. It is better to delete some color now than after the layout reaches the printer. Be careful that your color layout does not call for close registration with black copy (except where special

art work or color mats are prepared for registration) without first consulting the printer and pressman.

(6) When the layout is complete, spray it with fixative to make sure it stays neat and fresh. If changes are required later, don't attempt to erase. Paste a piece of paper over the area to be changed and re-do.

Do's and Don'ts in Color Application

It is undesirable to print a halftone photograph or illustration over color unless a special color plate has been made for that purpose. A halftone, if printed over a screened color area, often produces a Moray (a dot pattern that breaks up the quality of the picture). However, halftone illustrations can sometimes produce good effects if double-printed (the illustration is printed in color and again in black). This should not be used with photographs or any illustration in which the detail is important. Generally speaking, it is unwise to print any kind of important illustration in color alone. Color does not reproduce as faithfully as black in these cases, and the effectiveness is reduced. If you desire to combine color with an illustration, consult an artist or ask your mat service representative to provide you with kits complete with instructions for this purpose. Some excellent glue-backed materials are available that can be cut out and pasted on mats to obtain color plates that will match exactly the illustrations you have chosen.

Do not lay out an ad with irregularly shaped blocks or areas unless you provide a template or mat for casting. Consult your printer about this.

If using color areas under printed type, leave wide margins of color around the type to avoid confusion in reading. Except in large headings, you should never let the type cover both colored and white areas. Experience and judgment will train you in most of these matters.

Some Facts About Color
- Gradations between black and white are *tones.*
- Hue is the *name* of the color.
- Tint is the *lighter variety* of the color.
- Shade is the *darker variety* of the color.

- Red, orange, yellow are *warm* colors.
- Blue, green, violet are *cool* colors.
- Complementary colors, shades, tints make up *deficiencies*.
- Analogous colors are *similar* to each other.

Appendix

APPENDIX A

Examples of advertising masquerading as news, clipped from high-school and college publications, edited to eliminate identification:

All yell leaders, song girls, and interested Megaphone members are urged to attend the umpteenth annual Cheerleaders Clinic from 9 A.M. until 3 P.M. Saturday, March 13, at XYZ High School.

John J. Doe, executive secretary of the National Cheerleaders Association, will be the primary leader of the clinic, and the program will be under his direction.

Price of the clinic, which includes registration fee and box lunch, is $2.25. Tickets for the Northern California Invitational Basketball Tournament Saturday evening may be purchased for 50¢ extra.

All prospective and present cheerleaders may see Mrs. Roe for reservations.

The XYZ High School graduation party being held June 12 has a new attraction. It was recently announced by XYZ Amusement Company that arrangements have been made with the ABC Motor Company to award a Blip Blip automobile as a special grad night prize at each of the four all-night parties.

The graduation nights at XYZ, now a tradition, will take place June 11, 12, 18, and 19. Seniors and their dates from more than 120 high schools will attend the festivities in the Magic Kingdom.

The four Blip Blip autos to be given away will be white with red leather upholstery. Deluxe extra equipment includes 289-h.p. 4-vent engine, 4-speed manual transmission, seat belts, push-button radio, and other conveniences.

Highlight of each of the parties will undoubtedly be the announcement of the winner of the new car.

The end of the month is approaching at tremendous speed, and along with January 31 comes the end of the annual sale. That will definitely be the last day that a student may purchase a copy of the yearbook. So a word to the wise should be sufficient. Get yours now or be sorry!

Annuals can be purchased any day of the week at the Accountant's office during lunch periods. The price is $4.50 with student body card and $5.50 with an ID card.

The Annual staff will order only the number of Annuals that are sold as of the 31st. They will be delivered June 7.

Tonight's Valentine dance in the cafetorium is being sponsored by the publications department. Admission to the dance, entitled "Silhouettes in Red," is 50¢ with student body card and $1 without. Bring your sweetheart and come to this dance. Get your tickets now at the cashier's office. They will not be available tonight.

APPENDIX B

HOW TO SURVEY YOUR MARKET

The Questionnaire (A) should be carefully planned to include all information peculiar to the school and community. That which is not the custom should be omitted. Nor should any item intended to amuse be permitted. The project is a serious undertaking and should be so regarded by everyone concerned. The findings are vital to the construction of the advertising presentation and may be of value to courses other than Journalism, such as Business or Economics, or to school administration.

Distribution and collection of the Questionnaire should be rigidly supervised. It should be completely explained to the principal, public information officer, student body government, or whatever authority is involved, whose full co-operation will be essential.

The best time for distribution is during home-room, study, or if possible, a class. Plenty of time should be allowed for filling out the form, and students should be admonished to do so honestly.

The advertising staff should count and tabulate the findings and compute the percentages, using a summary sheet such as the suggested format (B). The editor should share this experience. Final calculations should be checked by the adviser and school accountant. Accuracy is most important.

Besides being the backbone of the advertising sales presentation for school publications, the statistics produced by the survey will prove to be source material for many interesting feature stories and editorials, especially as the year-to-year sequence develops and then-and-now comparisons become possible.

Especially significant will be news releases to the local community newspaper. The summary sheet will provide material for several stories that will reflect the composition of the school and make an impression on lay, professional, and business segments of the public.

For example, the number of students who work to help with current expenses or to save money for future education creates a good impression of the school as being populated with ambitious students. The businessman reading this is apt to look upon the school publication as having the kind of readership that will be of benefit to him. All in all, publicity of the results of the Purchasing Power Questionnaire will greatly enhance the reputation of the school in its community.

(A) *Suggested Purchasing Power Questionnaire*

Directions: Please study carefully, and fill in the following sheet accurately. Do not sign your name or otherwise identify it in any way. Turn it in to administrator when finished.

From　(Name of publication)
Room　(Number- name of school)
　　　　(Street, City, State)

Boy _____　Girl _____　Age _____　Grade _____

Weekly allowance $_____
Weekly earnings $_____　Home _____　Outside home _____

Part-time _____　Summer _____

Do you have a personal charge account? _____
Do you use your parents' charge account? _____
Do you have a personal savings account? _____
　　Purpose? Higher education _____　Career _____　Other _____
Did you select your savings bank? _____
Same as parents'? _____　Different? _____　Why? _____

Do you have insurance? _____　Do you own a car? _____
Motorcycle? _____　Bicycle? _____　Motor Scooter? _____
Typewriter? _____　Radio? _____　Record Player? _____
Boat? _____

I. Purchasing Power

I buy the following of my own choice with my own money for my own use:

_____ Stationery, greeting cards
_____ Lunches off campus
_____ Gifts
_____ Candy
_____ Ice cream
_____ Haircuts
_____ Hair styling
_____ Records
_____ Musical instrument
_____ Jewelry
_____ Camera
_____ Darkroom and developing supplies
_____ Photographic film
_____ Photo developing
_____ Deodorants
_____ School supplies
_____ Luggage
_____ Photographic portrait
_____ Books
_____ Magazines
_____ Trips (without family)
_____ Summer camp tuition
_____ Lessons (music, dance, skiing, flying, etc.)
_____ Tutorial services
_____ Lecture notes
_____ Toothpaste
_____ Soft drinks
_____ Tickets (movies, plays, sports events, etc.)
_____ Dues, fees (club, sorority, fraternity)
_____ Hi-Fi
_____ TV
_____ Radio
_____ Tape recorder and tapes
_____ Pets, pet supplies
_____ Bicycle
_____ Automobile
_____ Hobby materials
_____ Sports equipment

_____ Gasoline, oil
_____ Tires, accessories
_____ Motorcycle
_____ Motor scooter
_____ Phonograph
_____ Shoe-care supplies

II. BOYS PLEASE CHECK (In addition to the above)

_____ Shoeshines
_____ Shaving cream
_____ Razor blades
_____ Razor
_____ Suits
_____ Topcoats
_____ Jackets
_____ Shirts
_____ Slacks
_____ Ties
_____ Jeans
_____ Belts
_____ Socks
_____ Underwear
_____ Shoes
_____ Hats
_____ Beachwear
_____ Tux rentals
_____ Taxi fare
_____ Corsages
_____ Tools
_____ Wallets

GIRLS PLEASE CHECK

_____ Personal products
_____ Cosmetics, facials
_____ Manicure supplies
_____ Hairsprays
_____ Shampoos
_____ Home permanents
_____ Hand lotions
_____ Curlers
_____ Coats

_____ Dresses
_____ Knitting supplies
_____ Sewing supplies
_____ Fabrics
_____ Sweaters
_____ Skirts
_____ Slacks
_____ Shorts
_____ Pedal pushers
_____ Hosiery
_____ Lingerie
_____ Sleepwear
_____ Scarves
_____ Belts
_____ Bags
_____ Furs
_____ Hope chests

III. Family Shopping

Do you shop? _____ Do you assist? _____
Do your opinions influence the purchases of your family? _____

What kind of advertising influences your choices?
Newspaper _____ Radio _____ TV _____ Magazine _____
Billboard _____ Bus posters _____ Window displays _____

(B) Suggested Fact Summary Sheet

Total Respondents	Boys	Girls	12	13	14	15	16	17	18	19	20	21	22	23	24	25

EARNINGS: ALLOWANCES:
    Weekly average $_____   Weekly average $_____

NUMBER WHO WORK: Boys   Girls

        Part time   _____   _____
        Summer   _____   _____

Number of personal savings accounts _____

Number who have selected own banks _____
    "   "   use parents' banks   _____
    "   "   have insurance   _____
    "   "   own typewriter   _____
    "   "   own bicycle   _____
    "   "   own motor scooter _____
    "   "   own motorcycle   _____
    "   "   own hi-fi   _____
    "   "   own radio   _____
    "   "   own phonograph   _____
    "   "   own boat   _____

I. PURCHASING POWER

Percentage of students buying the following for their own use with their own money:

(Repeat here the items under I, II, and III in Questionnaire preceded by the percentage.)

APPENDIX C

BUREAU OF ADVERTISING, ANPA, "TELL IT TO THE TEENS" BUYING POWER SURVEY 1956

	Teens buy their own
Records	57%
Fountain pens	55
Jewelry	40
Shoes	36
Deodorants	34

	Teens selecting
Shoes	94%
Fountain pens	80
Sports equipment	70
Radios	55
Shampoos	52
Watches	47
Vacations	38

	Boys selecting
Shirts and slacks	90%
Shaving cream	49
Razor blades	35
Electric razors	26

	Girls selecting
Blouses and skirts	94%
Dresses	92
Lipstick	92
Lingerie	89
Hand lotion	91
Toilet soap	56
Permanents	33

APPENDIX D-1

BUSINESSES LIKELY TO ADVERTISE
IN SCHOOL PUBLICATIONS

Clothing sales and rentals
Amusements
Nonalcoholic beverages
School plays, athletic events, class concessions, dances, office seekers, etc.
Phonograph records
Musical instruments, supplies
Drugs, sundries
Barbers and beauty shops
Sporting goods
Florists
Radio and hi-fi
Jewelers
Gifts
Stationery and school supplies
Photography supplies
Optometrists
Food
Books
Printing shops
Bicycle, motorcycle, scooter, and auto agencies
Banks, savings institutions, lending agencies
Portrait studios
Restaurants
Auto parts, tires
Educational institutions
Public stenographers, typists

Lecture notes
Bakeries
Candy stores
Cleaners and dyers
Dance studios
Department stores
Service stations
Hardware
Shoe repair
Sewing fabrics and supplies
Sewing machines
Greeting cards
Auto driving schools
Trophies, gavels, plaques
Employment agencies
Travel agencies
Fashion shows
Theaters
Sororities, fraternities, off-campus social clubs
Typewriter sales and service
Luggage and leather goods
Art supplies
Pet supplies
Variety stores
Cosmetic studios

APPENDIX D-2

SEASONAL AND INSTITUTIONAL SELLING EVENTS

January
March of Dimes
United Cerebral Palsy Month
International Printing Week
National Jaycee Week
YMCA Week
National Fur Care Week

February
Valentine's Day
National Sickroom Needs
Month
American Heart Month
Boy Scout Week
National Electrical Week
National Beauty Salon Week
Defense Week
National Engineers' Week
Brotherhood Week

March
St. Patrick's Day
Red Cross Fund
Children's Art Month
Save Your Vision Week
Easter Seal Appeal
Girl Scout Week

Campfire Girls Anniversary
National Wildlife Week

April
Easter
Arts and Crafts Week
National Hobby Month
Cancer Crusade
Let's All Play Ball
Hardware Week
National Library Week
YWCA Week
National Garden Week

May
Mother's Day
National Foot Health Month
Clean-up, Paint-up, Fix-up Time
Ice Cream Festival
American Bike Month
Better Hearing Month
Home Improvement Month
Be Kind to Animals Week
Let's Go Fishing
National Frozen Foods Week
Brand Names Week

169

June
Father's Day
National Recreation Month
Let's Play Golf
National Swim-for-Health Week
Let's Play Tennis
National Safe Boating Week

July
Independence Day
National Hot Dog Month

August
Back to School
National Sandwich Month
Coast Guard Day (4th)
Aviation Day (19th)
V.J. Day (14th)

September
Better Breakfast Month
Lighting Fixture Month
Child Foot Health Month
Labor Day
National Child Safety Week
National Home Week
Citizenship Day (17th)
Constitution Week
National Sweater Week
National Chiropractor Day
  (18th)
Jewish New Year
National Tie Week
National Dog Week
Fall begins
American Indian Day (27th)
Gold Star Mother's Day (30th)

October
United Fund
National Restaurant Month
Science Youth Month
Fire Prevention Week
National Business Women's
  Week
Employ the Physically
  Handicapped Week
National Pharmacy Week
Letter-Writing Week
Hallowe'en
Columbus Day
National Newspaper Week
Thrift Week
Sweetest Day
U.N. Week
National Flower Week
Navy Day

November
Thanksgiving Day
International Aviation Month
International Cat Week
American Education Week
National Children's Book Week
Veterans Day
Youth Appreciation Week
Diabetes Week
National Farm-City Week
Know Your America Week

December
Chanukah
Christmas
New Year

APPENDIX E

TOOLS OF THE MARKETING MIX

Retail

I. Cost of merchandise

II. Store operating expense

   A. Administrative
      1) Executive
      2) Accounting
      3) Miscellaneous

   B. Merchandising
      1) Buying
      2) Selling

   C. Publicity
      1) Advertising
      2) Display

   D. Occupancy
      1) Rent
      2) Taxes

   E. Delivery

III. Income from sales

IV. Profit or loss

171

Wholesale

I. Concept of the Marketing Mix
   A. Market forces bearing on the mix

II. Elements of marketing
   A. Merchandising (sales planning)
   B. Packaging
   C. Pricing
   D. Branding
   E. Channels of distribution
   F. Physical handling
   G. Personal selling
   H. Servicing
   I. Sales promotion
   J. Research
   K. Advertising and display

APPENDIX F

Co-operative advertising is that for which the manufacturer or distributor pays part of the space costs, supplies the material, and dictates at least some of the conditions of its use. An example is the A-1 slacks ad reproduced here from the *Daily Jacket,* Berkeley (Calif.) High School. The Kotzin Company, manufacturer, pays a proportion, usually 50 per cent, of the cost of the space with exception of the signature. This is paid for wholly by Harris. The total amount over a period of time that will be paid by Kotzin is based on a percentage of the purchase of A-1 slacks by Harris.

When portraits of living models are used in advertising, a signed receipt and release should be obtained from them.

The form may be:

"I, the undersigned, living at _____,
do hereby declare that I am ___ years of age, and do hereby consent and have my parents' consent that _____
may use for advertising purposes and/or for the purposes of trade, my name, portrait, or other likeness.

	Signed _____
Date _____	Parent or guardian
City of _____	
State of _____	If over 21, signature of witness

In the case of the dead, "the right of privacy dies with the person." The statutory rights of the dead are not passed on to his relatives or representatives. It is good practice in advertising to refer legal problems to an attorney.

Some points to consider before using a photograph or other likeness in advertising are the following:

Be sure you have written consent from the photograph's owner or subject or both, for its use and/or use of subject's name.

Obtain in writing a guarantee that exclusive rights of publication have not been assigned to someone else.

Do not use a photograph or likeness that disparages or ridicules the subject or his business, trade, occupation, or hobby, or is libelous in any other way.

Make no representation that subject is a patron, customer, or user of product or service if this is not so.

APPENDIX H

The "big two" services for general advertising illustrations, mats, and reproduction proofs are:

Metro Associated Service, 80 Madison Ave., New York, New York 10016.

Stamps-Conheim-Whitehead, 555 North La Brea, Los Angeles, California, and 101 Fifth Avenue, New York, N.Y.

Among many specialized services on the market are:

Evans and Brisebois, Lafayette Bldg., Detroit, Michigan.

Multi-Ad Services, Inc., 100 Walnut St., Peoria, Illinois.

Famous Brand Promotions, Margate, New Jersey.

MacDonald Space Builder Service, Lafayette, Indiana.

Newspaper Enterprise Association, 1200 West Third St., Cleveland, Ohio.

"COLD-TYPE" METHODS AND MACHINES

"Cold type" is produced by methods other than that of being cast from molten metal.

For example, "hot type" comes from the Linotype, Intertype, Monotype, or Ludlow line-casting machines, and "cold type" is made by electronic or photographic processes.

Many cold-type machines are on the market and more in the pilot stage of development. Some utilize regular photographic film, others sensitized paper. Both electronic and light projection are used.

Some companies manufacture specialty units, others complete systems. For example, manufacturers of the Linotype and Intertype hot-type casting machines make all-inclusive photographic cold-type outfits consisting of camera, film developer, typesetter, composer, and corrector.

Individual firms make such specialty units as typesetters, recorders, reproducers, headline makers, cameras, presses, and plate-makers.

The cameras can take photographs of full-size newspaper pages from any angle and reduce or enlarge on almost any scale. Some of the photo typositor heading and headline machines feature instantaneous film development. The type image is transferred to a ribbon of film by operation of a keyboard, and the ribbon emerges at once with the lettering on it all ready for paste-up. In other methods the film must be developed from a negative in the usual manner.

A new substance called "conversion" film is a nonphotographic, pressure-sensitive film for transferring exact printing detail from letterpress forms to negatives for photo-mechanical plate-making.

New also are art projectors that make prescreened photos for offset production. No negative is needed to obtain a positive image from the original copy.

Many firms are now building offset and lithograph presses. They range from small-office reproducers on which many school publications can be and are printed to huge newspaper and magazine complexes.

The small- and medium-sized justifying typesetters and offset presses and duplicators are so simple and do such excellent work that there is hardly any excuse for a school to be without a publication.

APPENDIX J

RULES FOR BETTER TYPOGRAPHY

(1) Typewrite the copy, double- or triple-spaced, on one side of uniform-sized sheets of paper.

(2) Leave at least 1½-inch margin at left and right sides of each page and at least 2 inches at top.

(3) Type so that the right-hand margin is as even as possible.

(4) Type the same number of lines on every page.

(5) Never vary spacing. If you start with double spacing, keep all spacing double.

(6) Material may be indented from both sides if you want it to stand out.

(7) All paragraph indentations should be standard five spaces.

(8) Use a sturdy paper than can stand handling and will take pencil and ink.

(9) Carbon copies should never be used as originals, because they smudge.

(10) Correct copy carefully before it is set in type; "author's alterations" later are costly.

(11) If clippings, etc., must be used, paste them on standard-sized copy sheets.

(12) Number and title all pages consecutively, and on the last sheet write "end" or "30."

(13) If headings and captions are typed separately from the text, be sure to key the text with guidelines so that the compositor can place them with the proper copy or pictures.

(14) Be sure copy will fit the allotted area.

(15) Check carefully for uniform style, punctuation, spelling, capitalization, and figures—such as names, dates, prices, and statistics.

(16) Specify type face, point sizes, measures, indentations, lightface or boldface, spacing, number of proofs and when, or "printer's judgment."

(17) Furnish all copy and layout together.

(18) On the back of each picture, or on a tab pasted to it, write name of advertiser and advertising medium, size of illustration in the layout, how it is to be cropped or otherwise treated, date of insertion. Write lightly on backs of photos, so that indentation will not show on surface.

(19) Answer all proofreaders' queries.

(20) Mark corrections clearly in margins of proofs.

APPENDIX K

ACKNOWLEDGMENTS

Examples of advertising reproduced in this book were taken from various school publications as listed below:

Figs. 1, 2	Berkeley (Calif.) High School *Daily Jacket*
Fig. 3	Topeka (Kans.) High School *World*
Fig. 4	Berkeley (Calif.) High School *Daily Jacket*
Fig. 5	Missoula County (Mont.) High School *Konah*
Figs. 6, 7	Berkeley (Calif.) High School *Daily Jacket*
Fig. 8	Santa Rosa (Calif.) Junior College *Oakleaf*
Fig. 9	Berkeley (Calif.) High School *Daily Jacket*
Fig. 10	Seattle (Wash.) Roosevelt High School *News*
Fig. 11	Union City (Calif.) James Logan High School *Colt's Courier*
Figs. 12, 13, 14	Berkeley (Calif.) High School *Daily Jacket*
Fig. 15	Seattle (Wash.) Queen Anne High School *Kuay Weekly*
Figs. 16, 17	Berkeley (Calif.) High School *Daily Jacket*
Fig. 18	Chico (Calif.) High School *Red & Gold*
Fig. 19	Berkeley (Calif.) High School *Daily Jacket*
Fig. 20	Chico (Calif.) High School *Red & Gold*
Figs. 21, 22	Berkeley (Calif.) High School *Daily Jacket*
Fig. 23	Seattle (Wash.) Roosevelt High School *News*
Fig. 24	*Indianapolis* (Ind.) Shortridge High School *Daily Echo*
Figs. 25, 26	Berkeley (Calif.) High School *Daily Jacket*
Fig. 27	Pico Rivera (Calif.) El Rancho High School *El Rodeo*

183

GLOSSARY

Advertising. Descriptive, persuasive message whose purpose is to influence, convince, persuade, stir to action; a sponsored appeal to buy.

Agate Line. A unit measurement of publication advertising space one column wide (no matter what width) and 1/14 inch deep.

Bullet. Round, black type dot in front of a line in text.

Boldface. Heavy tone in type.

Body Type. Type used in main text of advertisement.

Caps. Capital letters.

Cold Type. Type derived from the various reproduction techniques and processes used in the offset printing method.

Copy. Written content of an advertisement.

Circulation. Number of copies of a publication distributed.

Composition. Typesetting.

Cropping. Trimming an illustration to fit a specific space or to eliminate nonessential portions.

Display. Advertising composed of type larger than body type and/or illustrations.

Dummy. A page design, showing placement of advertising in relation to editorial content.

Dead Metal. Spaces between illustrations in a mat sheet.

Engraving. A design etched into a metal plate, from which an exact impression is transferred to paper in the printing process.

Face. Style of type.

Gutter. Nonprinting space between facing type pages.

Halftone. Reproduction of illustration in metal with screen (dot) background for tonal distribution.

Hot Type. Type cast from molten metal by machines such as Ludlow, Monotype, Linotype, or Intertype.

Layout. Design of an advertisement depicting distribution of its elements.

Letterspace. Insertion of spacers between characters of type to make the line wider or more legible.

Medium (Pl. Media). Means by which a message is conveyed to readers: newspaper, magazine, yearbook, pamphlet, and the like.

Make-Up. Process of assembling type for printing.

Mat(rix). Impression of type, rule, illustration in a cardboardlike substance from which a metal reproduction cast is made.

Omnibus. Advertisement composed of several or many unrelated items.

Prospect. Client or consumer to whom the advertising or sales message is directed.

Proof. Reproduction in ink on paper of type, rule, or illustration.

Pegging. Setting of type by hand.

Registration. Exact coincidence of color with the area in the advertisement it is to occupy.

Retailing. Direct-to-consumer selling.

R.O.P. Run-of-paper position (anywhere in paper).

Straight Matter. Editorial content of publication.

Slug. A slab of metal, either with type cast on top for printing, or blank for spacing.

Signature. Name of firm sponsoring the advertisement.

Stick. Receptacle into which type is "pegged" by hand; to set type by hand.

Set to fill. Use type large enough to completely fill the line.

Space out. Spread lines wider apart to fill allotted space or to make them more legible.

Set solid. Place lines together closely as possible.

Tint Block. An area of solid color over which type is printed.

White Space. Blank areas in advertisement; more generally, any area of unprinted paper.

BIBLIOGRAPHY

Books

American Newspaper Publishers Association, Bureau of Advertising, "How to Check Your Ads for More Sell," 1957.

———— "Continuing Study of Newspaper Advertising."

———— "Time Table of Retail Opportunities."

Arnold, Arthur Carl and Powers, Robert H. *Advertising Type Combinations.* Detroit: Dragon Press, 1931.

Bedell, Clyde O. *How to Write Advertising That Sells.* New York: McGraw-Hill, 2nd edition, 1952.

Birren, Faber. *Color, Form and Space.* New York: Reinhold Publishing Corp., 1961.

Blaine, Stanley Thomas. *Advertising Typography.* New York: Prentice-Hall, 1935.

Borden, Neil H. and Marshall, Martin V. *Advertising Management: Text and Cases.* Revised edition. Homewood, Ill.: Richard D. Irwin, Inc.

Caples, John. *Advertising for Immediate Sales.* New York and London: Harper Bros., 1936.

————. *Tested Advertising Methods.* New York and London: Harper Bros., 1947.

De Lopatecki, Eugene. *Advertising Layout and Typography.* New York: Ronald Press Corp., 1935.

Doremus, William L. *Advertising for Profit.* New York and Chicago: Pitman Publishing Corp., 1947.

Duffy, Ben. *Advertising Media and Methods.* New York: Prentice-Hall, 1939.

Edwards, Charles M. and Brown, Russel A. *Retail Advertising and Sales Promotion.* Englewood Cliffs, N.J.: Prentice-Hall, Inc., 1959.

Hepner, Harry Walter. *Modern Advertising Practices and Principles.* New York: McGraw-Hill, 1956.

Hymes, David. *Production in Advertising and the Graphic Arts.* New York: Henry Holt & Co., 1958.

Kimberly Clark Corp. *Fundamentals of Printing.* Neenan, Wisconsin, 1958.

Kleppner, Otto. *Advertising Procedure.* Englewood Cliffs, N.J., Prentice-Hall, Inc., 4th edition, 1960. (This book contains an excellent list of books on all phases of advertising. See "Reading Suggestions," pages 710-719.)

Manville, Richard. *How to Create and Select Winning Advertisements, Pre-evaluation in Advertising.* New York and London: Harper Bros., 1947.

McCarthy, Helen M. E. *Advertising in School Publications.* New York: Columbia University Scholastic Press Association.

Marshall, Charles, et al. *How to Prepare Display Advertising.* San Jose (Calif.) State College Department of Journalism and Advertising.

McClure, Leslie. *Newspaper Advertising and Promotion.* New York and London, Macmillan Co., 1950.

Rivers, Donald T. *Your Career in Advertising.* New York: E. P. Dutton & Co., Inc., 1947.

Rowland, C. M. *Advertising in Modern Retailing.* New York: Harper Bros., 1954.

Sandage, C. H. (ed.). *The Role of Advertising.* Homewood, Illinois: R. D. Irwin, Inc., 1960.

Sandage, C. H. and Fryburger, Vernon. *Advertising: Theory and Practice.* (Fifth Ed.) Homewood, Illinois: R. D. Irwin, Inc., 5th ed., 1959.

Scott, Walter D. *The Psychology of Advertising.* Boston: Small, Maynard, 1921.

Strunk, William. *The Elements of Style.* New York: Macmillan Co., 1959.

Young, J. O. *Adventures in Advertising.* New York: Harper Bros., 1949.

Periodicals

Advertising Age, 200 East Illinois St., Chicago, Illinois.

American Printer, 48 West 38th Street, New York, New York 10018.

Columbia Journalism Review, 602 Journalism Bldg., Columbia University, New York, New York.

Editor and Publisher, 850 Third Ave., New York, New York.

Graphic Arts Monthly, 61 South Dearborn St., Chicago, Illinois 60605.

Industrial Marketing, 200 East Illinois Street, Chicago, Illinois 60611.

Inland Printer, 309 West Jackson Blvd., Chicago, Illinois 60606.

Journal of Marketing, 1525 East 53rd St., Chicago, Illinois.

Journalism Quarterly, Association for Education in Journalism, University of Iowa, Iowa City, Iowa.

Lineage, Official Organ, National Professional Advertising Fraternity, Department of Journalism, Southern Illinois University, Carbondale, Illinois.

Marketing, 119 York St., Toronto, Ontario, Canada.

Printers' Ink, 501 Madison Ave., New York, New York.

Printed Selling and Production, 22 East Huron St., Chicago, Illinois, 60611.

Quill and Scroll, School of Journalism, University of Iowa, Iowa City, Iowa.

Sales Management, 386 Fourth Ave., New York, New York.

Scholastic Editor, 18 Journalism Bldg. University of Minnesota, Minneapolis, Minnesota.

School Press Review, Columbia Scholastic Press Association, Columbia University, New York, New York.

Southern Advertising, 75 Third St., N.W., Atlanta, Georgia.

Southwestern Advertising and Marketing, Southland Life Bldg., Dallas, Texas.

Tide, 633 Madison Ave., New York, New York.

Western Advertising, 580 Market St., San Francisco, California.